THE MOST IMPORTANT WORK

*Stories of Sovereignty
in the Struggle for Literacy*

Edited by
Kyle D. Shanton

University Press of America,® Inc.
Lanham · Boulder · New York · Toronto · Plymouth, UK

Copyright © 2015 by
University Press of America,® Inc.
4501 Forbes Boulevard
Suite 200
Lanham, Maryland 20706
UPA Acquisitions Department (301) 459-3366

Unit A, Whitacre Mews, 26-34 Stannary Street,
London SE11 4AB, United Kingdom

All rights reserved

British Library Cataloging in Publication Information Available

Library of Congress Control Number: 2015938556
ISBN: 978-0-7618-6602-2 (paperback : alk. paper)
eISBN: 978-0-7618-6603-9

TABLE OF CONTENTS

Foreword — v

Introduction
Chapter One: Listening, Storytelling, and Literacy — 1

A Critical Literacy of Family Child Care Policy, Practice, and Self-Determination
Chapter Two: Improving Family Child Care: Navigating a Rugged Landscape of Concerns, Expectations, and Needs — 12
Chapter Three: "'You're doing the best with what you have.' 'No, we do with what we don't have.'" — 39
Chapter Four: Listening: A Channel for Critical Literacy — 48

Literacy Demands on New Mexico Teachers and Students: Context, Perspective, and Hope
Chapter Five: Demands of Official Portraits — 53
Chapter Six: Encountering New Demands—Composing Non-official Portrait — 62
Chapter Seven: Acting Upon, With, and For Literacy — 78

Reading the (De)Colonized World: Cultural Literacy for Pueblo of Laguna Students
Chapter Eight: Literacy from a Native Vantage Point — 86
Chapter Nine: The Laguna History and Culture Class — 95
Chapter Ten: Reclaiming the Laguna Worldview — 111
Chapter Eleven: Laguna Cultural Literacy — 117

Conclusion
Chapter Twelve:
A Gift at a Most Opportune Time — 119

FOREWORD

Myrtle Irene Welch, Buffalo State College

When educators collaborate by listening to one another and identifying connections among their distinct efforts, they can weave a vibrant tapestry of solidarity. Such creative and skillful efforts guide their individual focuses toward taking bold next steps together to share what they have learned from their work and each other. In this book, one early care practitioner, one school administrator, two tribal leaders, two classroom teachers with more than fifty elementary students, and three education scholars intertwine distinct threads of their work and, as a result, present compelling call to listen closely to stories of struggle in literacy education. Through clearly different approaches, in unmistakably different contexts, these stories present remarkably similar commitments to treading paths of the most important work for sovereignty in literacy education, via anti-oppressive frameworks for analyzing, doing, reflecting and understanding what is at stake and what can be accomplished.

The critical role struggle plays in enacting self-determination and sovereignty has been referred to many times over ever since Fredrick Douglass first articulated this idea in his speech, *If There Is No Struggle, There Is No Progress*, on West India Emancipation delivered at Canandaigua, New York on August 4, 1857. Douglass' speech is itself an illustration of the invaluable significance of the pursuit of literacy to not only participate in democracy but also challenge a nation to uphold its democratic ideas. Moreover, the ring of self-determination echoes loudly and clearly across and beyond his eloquent call for struggle in order to make progress toward liberty for all. As far back as the nineteenth century, advocates of progressivism for self, community and education also saw that sovereignty was indeed necessary in literacy. In this book, the term, struggle, is a similarly progressive and reverent concept, which frames stories that feature the unquestionable value of sovereignty in literacy. As editor, Kyle Shanton—teacher educator, literacy specialist, literacy advocate, and one aware of the oppressive means used to control teaching and learning—raises critical questions about self, culture, language, literacy, pedagogical practices, sovereignty and struggle through his design for this book. As if it were not enough to simply raise such important questions, he and his colleagues discuss these questions in believable and compelling terms: early care and education, writing in elementary school, and US history in high school. And, despite the different contexts and demographics of those involved, there is unity across the work presented in this book. Each of the contributors—whether via counter-narratives, portraits, or stories—engages the reader with the use of critically aesthetic and authoritative descriptions and analyses of how literacy is achieved by and for those involved in the struggle. And, each points to the decisive significance of sovereignty in composing literacy.

Likewise, it was a personal quest for literacy—which happened more by providence than by chance or coincidence—that gives me the opportunity to write the foreword for the *most important work* articulated in this book. I was mentored through doctoral candidacy by Kyle Shanton. His collaborative and collegial commitments and style caused a *stir* (Welch, 2011) within me to reflect and reconsider those who *allegedly struggle* with literacy. Consequently, we investigated and reflected together upon high school students who were labeled *struggling* readers. We shared ideas, questions and perspectives via storytelling about my teaching and dissertation research. Kyle Shanton adroitly and methodically scaffolded me through doctoral study, my first publication, and into the academy.

Not long after the work against forces that colonize and marginalize students, families, and teachers in the Mountain Standard Time Zone was concluded for this book, we both relocated to the Eastern Standard Time Zone. As I stepped forward into new territory, I forged a parallel path by collaborating with academics and professional educators, keeping a sharp focus on understanding the myriad of ways sovereignty informs and influences the development of literacy. This work led me to Uganda, East Africa; there elementary and high school students, their teachers, academics and university administrators and I collaborated to open access to all who would want to write: we constructed a writing center, something unprecedented in the university's history, to provide appropriate and needed space for such work, as well as the unmistakable welcome to all to present their literacy.

Then, again by providence, Kyle Shanton and I re-connected: we collaborated on our most recent commitments to uphold the sovereignty of language and literacy in teaching and learning. This work emerged out of our independent, but related, journeys across national boundaries (i.e., United States, Costa Rica, and Uganda East Africa), impelling us to see connections across contexts and experiences among teachers who labor tirelessly to support students to speak their languages and tell their stories. Through this work we renewed our understandings of the profound significance of listening and storytelling in teaching and learning, as well as, of course, sovereignty in literacy.

Although this book emphasizes the unmistakable role of praxis in what they all accomplished, sovereignty in literacy is equally, if not more clearly, salient. Expertly and skillfully, authors Kyle Shanton, Victoria Cadena, Richard Myers, Patia Morales and Barbara Hopkins and their fifth and sixth grade students, Jeannette Haynes Writer, Lee Francis, and Gilbert Sanchez escort the reader through an album of authentic portraits and stories of those who struggle for sovereignty in literacy education. Sovereignty points to what was sacred across such different contexts and its liberation from authoritative praxis. So, powerful portraits of culturally relevant and liberating literacy experiences demonstrate the possibility to reform educational policies into self-determining opportunities to achieve literacy. In the words of Kyle Shanton, "Prescribing language, and a particular approach to literacy, will not make things better for children and their families. This will not create literacy—and it will not leave *no child behind.*"

In *The Most Important Work*, varied voices resonate loud and clear the path they are taking towards making literacy work for them. Throughout these pages, the reader will recognize that while there is yet much work to be done, this book amplifies the view of possibilities for literacy education when we recognize that human beings possess knowledge and potential that both can indeed emerge intentionally out of their own individual lived experiences and sociocultural histories as well as lead them fluidly to new understandings of themselves, their contexts and how to advance their literacy by learning with and from others.

I believe you will find these stories unforgettable. Thus I encourage you now, as you read this book, to consider carefully the work you have done and will do in light of what is most important.

References

Douglass, F. (1857). Two Speeches: One on West India Emancipation, Delivered at Canandaigua, August 4, and the Other on the Dred Scott Decision, Delivered in New York, on the Occasion of the Anniversary of the American Abolition Society, May 1857. Syracuse, new York: Cornell University Library.

Welch, I. (2011). Welch, M.I. (January 2011). Different Is Not Deficit: A Philosophical View of Diversity and Identity. *The International Journal of Diversity in Organizations, Communities and Nations*, 11(1), 33-46.

INTRODUCTION

CHAPTER ONE
LISTENING, STORYTELLING, AND LITERACY

Kyle D. Shanton, Albion College

> The tension in Carmen's arm, the ferocity of her need, the poignancy of her large woman's hand drawing her letters with so much pressure that the paper rips—that image embodies in an elemental, gripping way ... a hunger for the word and the worlds that become accessible through the word, a hunger for the connection that comes from learning and sharing what we know, and a hunger so particular to us women for news from women who have gone farther down the road than we have gone. We want to know the story of how they did it, for there is an implicit permission and possibility that comes from hearing that story. (Alvarez, J., 2000; p. xii)

Julia Alvarez wrote these words in her preface essay to *The Writer on Her Work*, emphasizing that when we engage in struggle to speak our own words a desire is born in us to also connect to others around us to share these words as well as learn theirs. This desire leads us to search for and connect to others by listening to their stories of struggle. Listening, sharing language and creating literacy as we communicate to one another what we know and need to know also helps us move more fluidly across the landscapes of our struggles. By recalling how she leaned over the shoulder of Carmen, placed her hand with hers, and formed the letters of Carmen's name on a piece of paper, Alvarez illustrated the invaluable role of collaboration in the struggle for both learning and literacy. I point to this image to compel you to listen closely to the stories in this book about the sovereignty of connecting to and collaborating with others to create literacy.

The ethno-linguistic diversity of children and youth across this nation has increased steadily to the point that for the first time in the recorded history of *American schooling* (i.e., academic year 2014-15) self-identified Caucasian, or *White*, children and youth are no longer the majority (http://www.economist.com/news/united-states/21613277-new-white-minority). Since becoming a Spanish-English, bilingual elementary school teacher in 1985, I have watched fear swell and inundate efforts to find and allocate ample resources to support needed changes in public education in general—and literacy education more specifically (Berliner & Glass, 2014; Spring, 2013). Such fear significantly targeted public policy on teaching, learning and literacy, constraining it with test preparation and penalties for inadequate annual performance (e.g., *No Child Left Behind Act*, 2001), as well as turning requests for funding into a competition that pits states against one another (e.g., *Race to the Top*, 2009). Teaching, learning and literacy have been more recently marginalized by another political maelstrom of philanthropy and legislation that standardizes what K-12 students, in any state in the Union, should know and be able to do by the time they graduate from high school. These efforts have systematically reduced the number of those who can acquire access to resources and eliminated access to educational opportunities within particular communities (Ravitch, 2010). Almost without exception, teachers, children, youth and their families tell stories that resonate their despair and disappointment about the limits of what is now official literacy learning and teaching. Forced to sit and complete one-minute-timed tests of alphabet identification, phonetic articulation, non-sense word recognition and oral reading, at five particular intervals across the year, kindergarteners cry out in confusion or groan their bewildered frustration; third graders stop eating, and endure sleepless nights, in some cases for more than a week, as the time draws near for them to take standardized grade-level promotion tests in reading, writing and mathematics; and, seniors become disinterested, indolent, resistant and even unruly about the requirement to demonstrate what every high school graduate *should know and be able to do*. Tracing those responses back in time to similar situations, it is clear that the traditions of marginalizing teachers' and students' knowledge—and ascribing what should constitute curriculum, pedagogy, language and literacy—are being carried out in newly seductive ways (Goodman, et al., 2004; Nichols and Berliner, 2007). Its roots in the longstanding, taken-for-granted practice of colonizing this place we call *our* country, and especially native and under-represented peoples, are intricately woven into the fabric of its rhetoric (Edelsky, 1999; McCarty, 2002). As I have become more troubled about what has happened, I have had to ask myself, "What do I want to say? Who also wants to speak out? And, how can we work together?"

Learning About Responsibility and Voice in Struggle

Learning from activists, educators and community leaders—such as Vivian Gussin Paley (1989), Victor Villanueva (1993), Gloria Ladson-Billings (1994), Sonia Nieto (1999), Anne Haas Dyson (2003), and Linda Christensen (2009)—I have come to realize that I have a responsibility to take a stand with, but not for, those who are struggling for teaching, learning and literacy. To assume this kind of responsibility, I think, requires what bell hooks (1994) called transgression. That is, I need to take seriously hooks' question about the risk of circumscribing certain individuals and their lived experiences by constituting them as liabilities—because of class, gender, language, race and/or sexuality. I need to understand how I might limit the opportunities they have by identifying any differences as irregularities inherent in them. As hooks points out, struggling for teaching, learning and literacy is a transgressive act because, "[l]ike desire, language disrupts, refuses to be contained within boundaries. It speaks itself against our will, in words and thoughts that intrude, even violate, the most private spaces of mind and body." (p. 167) So, when someone acquires or advances teaching, learning and literacy, she would ostensibly dislocate the boundaries that had previously been drawn against and around her. For me, I must be critically self-reflective in order to act responsibly: I must pay attention to how I use language, in its multiple forms, and have courage to name issues of (in)justice and (in)equity in order to participate in this process.

My efforts to struggle for literacy, like Julia's, must happen in the ordinary moments and customary spaces of daily life (Shor, 1996; Hill Collins, 2000) and involve my participation with those who have been labeled liabilities. Such a process would require me to connect to someone else and, "... do more than simply mirror or address the dominant reality, ... There, in that location, [we] make [language] do what [we] want it to do. [We] take the oppressor's language and turn it against itself. [We] make [our] words a counter-hegemonic speech, liberating [our]sel[ves] in language." (hooks, 1994, p. 175) From this alternative perspective, then, the struggle for teaching, learning and literacy lies not in the challenge to policy but in the *implicit possibilities* that these are varied and textured engagements, a real struggle embodied in the lives and collective consciousness of those who seek to use these both for themselves and with others.

Encountering Struggles for Plurality

While I was involved in research on the implementation of a pilot training program, sponsored by a state office of child development, to "improve the quality of in-home family child care," I became alarmed by the potentially undermining consequences of policy mandates on preschool children. After only the second training session, I recognized a familiar problem: Children living in poverty, and learning English as a second language, were identified as deficient because *their families were not providing them access to proper language and knowledge*. This encounter was unexpected; and, my realization about the scope of this political crusade against local literacies[1] was equally startling. I began to see for the first time that early care providers were now being trained, specifically, to prepare young children (i.e., between birth and the age of 5) to be sufficiently ready for school. These family custodians were cautioned about encouraging children to be satisfied speaking their very own words, or imagining "the worlds that become accessible through the[ir] word[s]." Moreover, I could sense a growing "hunger for the connection that comes from learning and sharing what [they] know," because their ideas, although rhetorically solicited, were quickly relegated as subordinate to what had officially and programmatically been predetermined as what they needed. Like the federal and state policies imposed on K-12 teachers, a corollary state policy now defined a curriculum and domain for family child care—outlining what can and should happen to care for and educate children inside one's own home.

Participants and trainers were actually aware of these incongruities as they experienced them in the training sessions; however, I did not notice these in the same way. We were apprehensive to share our insights with each other. It took time for me to affirm my integrity toward them and what they cared about most: the welfare of young children. Touted as an opportunity to enrich their professional development and prepare children for school, the pilot project was actually a strategy to establish the need to legislate this training as mandatory for all family care providers and restrict access to state subsidized food programs if not completed. As weeks passed, we became ever more aware of the underlying ideology through continuous conversations. We realized together that we needed to decide what to do in the face of such tensions without jeopardizing young children's access to much needed resources. In retrospect, what stands out to me most about this experience is the relief and uncertainty we (i.e., participants, trainers, and researcher) all seemed to simultaneously experience as we engaged in the project.

Every time I think about what I heard and witnessed, I keep drawing the same conclusion: Prescribing language, and a particular approach to teaching, learning and literacy, will not make things better for children and their families. This will not improve teaching, learning and literacy—and it will not leave *no child behind*. Instead, I think about what children and families, teachers and learners, leaders and followers *do* together to create literacy. I think about focusing more on the labor involved in the act of creation and what that entails. I realize how shared struggle and regard for sovereignty embody permission for and the possibility and production of meaningful and remarkable teaching, learning and literacy.

Once I began to listen more closely to what trainers and participants were saying to each other, noticing the ways they were sharing their stories, I also began to ask myself: "What is my role in this situation? What is my responsibility given what was happening?" For me, this was a critical reflection, a defining moment. It compelled me to awaken my consciousness and open up my perspective.

Eventually I found the answer to my question. My role and responsibility were to labor with them: figuring out how to acknowledge the policy mandate for their purposes not those of the state and, at the same time, disrupt that propaganda by translating the ferocity of their need into a literacy of and with them. I saw my obligation, then, as one of responding affirmatively to an intentional call to connect and share, much like what Julia experienced in her collaboration with Carmen to write her name.

Coming to this conclusion, I found myself determined to engage bell hooks' challenge to use my own teaching, learning, language and literacy, in camaraderie and collaboration with that of others, to challenge the disregard for multiple local knowledge and literacies. I desired to make this the frame for my own work as a literacy researcher, teacher and advocate. In this process, a new sense of urgency has emerged. This has happened, through various iterations, at different times and in different ways, in dialogue with many different individuals. Several of whom, I have found, share these, and other similar, concerns, and who have also connected with different communities and groups to struggle for literacy and plurality.

Engaging in struggles for plurality

For me, there was an ontological turn, from being fixated in arrogant despair to imagining possibilities with hope and urgency. This change has prompted me to bring together a group of respected colleagues in order to compose a book about the copious, on-going efforts that we have been undertaking, in different ways, in our teaching and research. The four of us set out to study and make sense of our work with different struggles for literacy and plurality in the borderlands of pre- scribed teaching, learning and literacy. Our work involved rigorous and sensitive engagements of many different kinds with children, youth, families, elders, teachers, and advocates. Nonetheless, these varied endeavors are inextricably connected to one another in two important ways.

First, there is a collective intentionality to connect with practitioners and come to understand how they engage with children, youth and families and inscribe their own lives and literacies for purposes that matter to them. And, second, there is a shared theoretical commitment to follow in the footsteps trod by anti-colonial, feminist critical and other anti-oppressive teachers and researchers who frame their work in terms of solidarity (hooks, 2002) and sovereignty (Duran, 2006), rather than monolithic stipulations of authority and expertise.

Design of the Book

This is a collection of essays that narrate the desire and determination required to work side by side in struggle toward more meaningful and relevant way. These es- says feature how individuals and groups encounter struggles for sovereignty in dif- ferent ways, engage in such struggles differently and what they accomplish in doing so.

The book is organized as three series of essays—in which an academic scholar works with a practitioner, or community leader, on a particular struggle toward teaching, learning and literacy. Together they craft texts that portray the reflexive relationships involved in that endeavor. These dialogical essays then re-present the praxis emerging from their work together. For example, in the case of collaboration by two individuals, the first essay is a narrative from the perspective of the academ- ic scholar; the second is a narrative from that of the practitioner; and, the third, an inter-textual collaboration between both to narrate a synthesis of their collaborative praxis. Additionally, a conclusion is presented to synthesize the most salient find- ings and reflections across the three series, as well as pose critical questions for further consideration and future inquiry.

Series One—A Critical Literacy of Family Child Care Policy, Practice and Self-determination

Remaining focused on the image of Julia Alvarez and Carmen, in order to envision the emotional, intellectual and physical, as well as cultural, historical and sociopolit- ical, embodiment of struggles for literacy, this work centers on struggles encountered by Victoria Cadena, a bilingual family child care specialist, as she endeavored to provide mandated training for in-home family care providers, who were predominantly elder, Spanish speaking, women. The aim of the training was to improve the quality of early care and build sound literacy foundations for children in rural borderlands. The purpose of this participatory inquiry was to try to understand the nature of these struggles and the ways that Victoria and the child care providers she worked with had to transgress (hooks, 1994) their practices and transform themselves.

Improving Family Child Care: Navigating a Rugged Landscape of Concerns, Expectations and Needs

Because these struggles had become even more pronounced with the hierarchically ascribed literacy values of the universal preschool child care curriculum recently legislated by the state—a statute that set confined conditions on the possibilities for these women to remain family child care providers and continue their work, Kyle Shanton questioned the taken-for-granted understanding of *para los niños* (i.e., for the children) by participating in the conversation-based professional development sessions with Victoria Cadena on this question and her work. He examines the contradictory texture of this rhetoric and how it denies the critical work already being done by women family child care providers all across the borderlands, as well as disavows the language and literacy of this place.

"'You're doing the best with what you have.' 'No, we do with what we don't have'."

Victoria Cadena writes about the many conversations with early care providers on the legislated mandates for training for them as well as her place in the midst of such politics. She envisions a *praxis* for addressing the demands of the law and her sense of being true to what these women and their communities want for their children. She narrates the journey she forged in providing the training course, and she poses her own questions about the idea of what is known about literacy and what all children should have and be able to do, turning her attention to alternative ideas for engendering literacy among the children in the care of different family child care providers.

Listening: A Channel for Critical Literacy

Kyle and Victoria consider the key role listening played in both the professional development conversations and the research approach. They describe and explain listening as a way to analyze and synthesize differences among policy, practice and perspective. Further, they point to the power of self-determination in transforming an essentialist focus on what is wanted into a much more comprehensive understanding of what and how individuals and groups can examine their needs and imagine goals for creating meaningful, successful and culturally relevant processes of teaching, learning and literacy.

Authors

Kyle Shanton is Associate Professor and Chair of Education at Albion College where he teaches courses in processes for understanding teaching and learning, literacy education, pedagogy of the humanities and *boundary crossing* in schools. Dr. Shanton's research interests include issues of language choice and use in teaching and learning, progressive forms of pedagogy, and education as a practice of freedom.

Ms. Victoria Cadena is a Family Child Care Specialist at *La Visión Institute*, a publicly funded Technical Training and Assistance Project of the state Child Youth and Families Department.

Section Two—Literacy Demands on New Mexico Teachers and Students: Context, Perspective and Hope

This series of chapters borrows from Sarah Lawrence-Lightfoot's (1997) portraiture to re-present images of how literacy education is being standardized as an official practice by policy makers for all teachers and children in a southwestern state. Narratives about the differences between official and non-official (or counter) portraits are crafted to challenge the official view of children, their language and culture and their literacy performance.

Demands of Official Portraits

Official portraits are created and framed by those in power (e.g., school district administrators, public education department officials, legislative policy makers) with the ultimate goal of satiating the demands of a politically dominant ideology that subjugate children, teachers, and the broader general public. Official portraits have specific goals. With an aim to magnify the pictures of literacy education across the state, and in order to specify the dangers that lurk in the details which remain largely broad stroked and homogenized by the official rhetoric, Richard Meyer examines how the state perpetuates its control, prolongs and cultivates compliance, and disrupts the possibilities for teachers and children in public schools to be able to enculturate their settings with commitments to democratic thinking and practice. Moreover, he discusses New Mexico as an exemplar of the danger of official portraits specific to and bounded by hierarchical policies.

Engaging the Demands—Composing Non-official Portraits

Additionally, data ignored by bureaucracy (i.e., poverty, suicide, alcohol and drug abuse, malnutrition) as a way of suggesting that the deficits attributed to children and teachers are more indicative of other relevant issues, such as health care, children's nutrition, and access to other services often taken for granted is presented. This narrative describes and explains the process by which Richard, teachers, and students engaged each other to craft non-official portraits of literacy in their school and community. Stories of two "unofficial" literacy projects, in which students' and teachers' conscientization (Freire 1970) led to the composition and appropriation of their own counterportraits, are narrated and used as pen sieves for critical reflection and hope.

Acting Upon, With and For Literacy

Based on the experiences of writing counterportraits, Richard Meyer, Patia Morales, Barbara Hopkins and the fifth and sixth graders in their two classes opened up possibilities for taking action to sustain changes in the overall quality of life in and out of school. This synthesis makes most clear the need for sustained relationships between teachers, students, and their families, as well as professional educators. It also reflects clearly the hegemonic nature of school and its powerful influence on teachers who lack a strong belief in teacher as decision-maker. Collaboration, however, is one way to strive for hope in the swirl of such powerful forces.

Authors

Richard Meyer is Professor of Language, Literacy and Sociocultural Studies at the University of New Mexico. He taught young children for nearly twenty years before earning his doctorate. Rick imagined spending most of his time with children in classrooms, their teachers, and their families; however, political realities have shifted his focus to work as an advocate for democratic teaching and learning in the face of repressive state and federal literacy policy.

Patia Morales teaches fifth grade and Barbara Hopkins teaches sixth grade Spanish-English bilingual students at Mesa Vista Elementary School.

Series Three—Reading the (De)Colonized World: Cultural Literacy for Laguna Students

In viewing Paulo Freire and Donaldo Macedo's (1987) concept of *reading the word, reading the world*, Jeanette Haynes Writer, Lee Francis and Gil Sanchez write about the struggle and pathway engaged by community members and educators within Laguna Pueblo to develop a curriculum for the Laguna History and Culture class at Laguna-Acoma High School. The class centers on Laguna Pueblo culture and history, as well as a conceptualization of education by and for the students and their community.

Literacy from the Native Vantage Point

Westernized education in terms of policies, curriculum and pedagogy has been imposed on Native Peoples for generations through on-going colonization. The Westernized system of education has served neo-colonial purposes to disregard and suppress the sovereign status of Native Nations. It has also seriously constricted self-determination. In this section, Jeanette presents an overview of Westernized education on Indigenous Peoples in the United States, presents background on her work with Lee and Gil, and the emergence of this story and its methodology.

The Laguna History and Culture Class

In this section stories of the history and process of developing the Laguna cultural literacy curriculum and what was expected to be achieved are told. These stories feature curriculum content information, concepts, and pedagogical philosophies and practices instilled in the course design. A few examples of program implementation in the community high school are highlighted. The local politics surrounding the implementation of the course are examined as well.

Reclaiming the Laguna Worldview

The development of the Laguna History and Culture class was important because the class clarified that culture is not just language and religion, but also it is all things that Laguna people are and were. Creating the class was a great learning experience for Gil, Lee and students. The lack of institutional resources and support did not halt the process of creating, teaching and learning. Background on the course curriculum was situated within the Laguna culture, history, language and people—community members were invested in the course and reflected Laguna community cultural wealth.

Laguna Cultural Literacy

In this section we discuss colonization, decolonization, sovereignty, and self-determination so we may begin to envision a critically and culturally altered educational path. We interrogate Freire and Macedo's (1987) idea of *reading the word, reading the world* from the Native perspective as we critique the written word of the Westernized education system for its continued imposition of inaccurate, and often times inappropriate, information about Native Peoples.

We see the development of the Laguna History and Culture class curriculum as centered on Laguna history, concepts, philosophies, pedagogy, and ideas of what it means to be a culturally literate Laguna Pueblo member. By envisioning Laguna Pueblo culture and history at the center, students and community members are able to *read the word and the world* in ways which create a space for community voice, develops individual and community strengths, fosters decolonization, and upholds sovereignty.

Authors

Jeanette Haynes Writer is Tsalagi (citizen of Cherokee Nation); she returns often during the academic year, and spends time each summer back home in Oklahoma, so she may participate in traditional ceremonial activities and maintain connection to her tribal community. Jeanette is Associate Professor and Head, Department of

Curriculum and Instruction at New Mexico State University, where she teaches undergraduate and graduate courses on multicultural education as well as curriculum and pedagogy. She developed and taught the university's first Indigenous education course and a course on Native Women through the Women's Studies Department. Jeanette's research interests and scholarly publications focus on Tribal Critical Race Theory, critical multicultural teacher education, social justice education, and Indigenous education.

Lee Francis (Laguna Pueblo of New Mexico) received his master's degree in Educational Leadership from the University of New Mexico in 2008 and is completing his PhD in Education at Texas State University. Lee is the current National Director of Wordcraft Circle of Native Writers and Storytellers. He previously served as the Executive Director of the Pueblo of Laguna Education Foundation and the Youth Development Coordinator for Laguna Partners For Success. Lee developed the curriculum and taught the Laguna History and Culture class at Laguna-Acoma High School and also assisted in the development of the College Preparatory Course for the Native American Community Academy in Albuquerque. He is an accomplished performer and award winning poet; his most recent work can be seen in *How To: Multiple Perspectives on Creating a Garden, a Life, Relationships and Community* by the Harwood Arts Press.

Gilbert Sanchez is of Laguna/Jemez Pueblo Indian decent, and is a tribal member from the Pueblo of Laguna. In 1992, he worked to establish the Pueblo of Laguna Department of Education—the first tribal operated education system in New Mexico; he then served as Program Officer for the New Mexico Community Foundation from 2007 to 2012 with a focus on the tribal communities. Gilbert currently serves as the Executive Director of the new Laguna Community Foundation, a non-profit 501c3 fundraising and grant-making organization that is not a tribal entity. He is returning to Pueblo of Laguna to establish a new foundation that will support community development efforts; and, he brings more than 35 years of award-winning educational leadership and philanthropic experience to lead this exciting endeavor.

Conclusion

Donna Muncey writes the conclusion both as a reiteration of the specific insights, issued by each of the contributors, and as a synthesis of what these mean for sustaining on-going struggles for sovereignty in literacy. She emphasizes the opportunity these inquiries present to learn from central and critical educative topics, such as family child care and the education of family child care providers, Pueblo of Laguna's history and cultural literacy and their *place* in the education of the Pueblo's students, and the learning and sense-making an educational community can do through creating poetry, or other literary forms. Moreover, she explains how these examples provide insight and guidance toward improving teaching and learning for all students, as well as toward more authentically engaging parents and members of a community in planning and creating education opportunities, which honors the power and promise of sovereignty in such struggle.

Author

Donna Muncey is a cultural anthropologist by training. After studying school reforms as instances of social and cultural change for over twenty years, she currently serves as a Senior Administrator in the Los Angeles Unified School District.

References

Alvarez, J. (2000). Preface. In J. Sternburg (Ed.), *The writer on her work*. New York: Norton & Company, Inc.

Berliner, D. & Glass, G. (2014). *50 Myths and Lies That Threaten America's Public Schools: The Real Crisis in Education*. New York: Teachers College Press.

Dewey, J. (1938; 1997). *Experience and education*. New York: Touchstone.

Duran, E. (2006). *Healing the soul wound: Counseling with American Indians and other Native Peoples*. New York: Teachers College Press.

Edelsky, C. (Ed.) (1999). *Making justice our project: Teachers working toward critical whole language practice*. Urbana, IL: NCTE.

Freire, P. & Macedo, D. (1987). *Literacy: Reading the word and the world*. Westport, CT: Greenwood Publishing.

Gonzalez, N., Moll, L & Amanti, C. (2005). *Funds of knowledge: Theorizing practices in households and classrooms*. Mahwah, NJ: Lawrence Erlbaum.

Goodman, K., Shannon, P., Goodman, Y., & Rappoport, R. (Eds.) (2004). *Saving our schools The case for public education, saying "no" to No Child Left Behind*. Berkeley, CA: RDR Books.

Hill Collins, P. (2000). *Black feminist thought: Knowledge, consciousness and the politics of empowerment*. New York: Routledge.

hooks, b. (1994). *Teaching to transgress*. New York: Routledge.

hooks, b. (2002). *Communion: The female search for love*. New York: Routledge.

Lakoff, G. (2002). *Moral politics: How liberals and conservatives think*. Chicago, IL: University of Chicago Press.

Lawrence-Lightfoot, S. & Hoffman-Davis, J. (1997). *The art and science of portraiture*. San Francisco: Jossey Bass.

Marmon Silko, L. (1996). *Yellow Woman and a beauty of the Spirit*. New York: Touchstone.

O'Hanian, S. (2001). *Caught in the middle: Nonstandard kids and a killing curriculum*. Portsmouth, NH: Heinemann.

Shor, I. (1996) *When students have power: Negotiating authority in a critical pedagogy*. Chicago: University of Chicago Press.

Spring, J. (2013). *Political Agendas for Education: From Race to the Top to Saving the Planet (Sociocultural, Political, and Historical Studies in Education)*. New York: Routledge.

Sternburg, J. (Ed.) (2000). *The writer on her work*. New York: Norton & Company, Inc.

Valenzuela, A. (2000). *Leaving children behind: How "Texas-style" accountability fails Latino youth*. Albany, New York: State University of New York Press.

Notes

[1] Literacies here is used in reference to the diverse ways in which multiple meanings are desired, shared, and negotiated.

SERIES ONE

A CRITICAL LITERACY OF
FAMILY CHILD CARE POLICY, PRACTICE,
AND SELF-DETERMINATION

CHAPTER TWO
IMPROVING FAMILY CHILD CARE:
NAVIGATING A RUGGED LANDSCAPE
OF CONCERNS, EXPECTATIONS, AND NEEDS

Kyle D. Shanton, Albion College

In-home child care—provided by either the child's own extended family, friends or neighbors—is the most widely used form of child care in the United States today (Children's Defense Fund, 2005; NARA & NCCITAC, 2009). Beyond the 22% of children who remain in their parent's or guardian's care on a daily basis, approximately 50% of the nation's infants, toddlers and preschool age children (i.e., between three and five years old) are believed to be in some form of *kith and kin* child care (i.e., in-home care provided by a family member, relative or friend of the family). This is due largely to a mix of two key factors: the affordability of such care[1], and the increasing number of working families living in poverty who require full-day care for their pre-school age children[2]. It is, then, critically important to emphasize the fact that the percentage of children in in-home child care situations has increased in direct relation to the rise in number of families living in poverty.

While various kinds of financial subsidy for in-home child care have been available for some time—largely through federal appropriations, such as Aid to Families With Dependent Children (1935-1996) and Temporary Assistance for Needy Families (1996-present)—and child advocates as well as politicians have attempted to promote beneficial change through policy initiatives, there remain serious concerns about the quality of in-home early child care. One such concern is related to the differences in state licensing regulations across the country. Because of these differences in licensure requirements, and types of authorization (e.g., licensed, registered, unregulated), it is especially difficult to ascertain the actual number of child care providers of, and the number of children in, such care. Moreover, assessing the needs of these providers and the children they care for in order to support them in gaining access to appropriate human and social services is equally challenging.

In-home kith and kin child care providers do not usually consider the work they do to be professional, nor do they see themselves as professionals. And they often refer to the care they provide as babysitting. For those who provide in-home care that is not subject by law to licensing regulations, it is common to work long hours, earn less than federal regulation of minimum wage, be isolated from contact with other adults doing similar work, and have no experience in professional development. Not surprisingly, questions about how to reach out to these individuals and improve the quality of in-home child care—especially in terms of school readiness—have recently become a priority. Attention to this has intensified in states all across the country because of the annually escalating numbers of children who receive this kind of care. However, reviews of the literature and surveys of current need—whether conducted in the interest of private foundation philanthropy (Annie E. Casey Foundation, 1999), government legislation (National Institute of Child Health and Human Development, 1998) or academic research (Shonkoff and Phillips, 2000; Love et al., 2003; Gonzalez-Mena, J., 2012)—indicate there are few examples of successful efforts to reach out to in-home kith and kin childcare providers in culturally and professionally responsive ways. In this chapter, I describe and examine a remarkably compelling and explicitly elaborated effort by family child care professionals to design and develop a culturally and professionally responsive model of service and support.

A Closer Look at In-home Family Child Care

Emerging out of longstanding concerns held by state officials, as well as changes in federal policy to further standardize early child care, in-home early child care development became a centerpiece of the Southwest State Home Provider Initiative (HPI) in 2001. Charlas was an 18 clock hour pilot professional development course of the Sharing Learning Opportunities (SLO) Project, sponsored by the Southwest State Child Youth and Families Department (CYFD) for in-home family child care providers (2003-2005). The purpose was to design and trial test a model for training family in-home child care providers in order to improve the quality of early child care in Southwest State.

The main strategy was to bring in-home child care providers together on a regular basis to discuss issues and topics relevant to both their work and state policy. Participants developed socio-cultural, discursive practices by reflecting on their questions and understandings through narrative (i.e., stories of various kinds) and using a dialogic process (i.e., back and forth exchanges within and around stories) to shape their professional conversations. Given this conceptualization of Charlas, I relied on both dialogue (Bakhtin, 1981; hooks, 1994; Marmon Silko, 1993) and narrative to compose a conceptual and theoretical framework for this research (Alverman, 2000; Barone, 2007; Chase, 2005; Clandenin & Connelly, 2000; Shanton & Valenzuela, 2005). My purpose, then, was to listen to as many of the different stories told and retold by those involved in the project and use story to understand how participants' made sense of child care issues and the Charlas model. This required what Clandenin and Connelly called "living life on the landscape." (p. 77) This is important because the inquiry itself is not simply a matter of looking for and recording stories. Rather, it was a labor of taking time to figure out who the participants were, what they had to say and how I would use this. Often this meant accommodating repeated efforts to tell stories and confirm that these were understood, especially given the particular situation. Such a conceptualization of narrative is itself dialogic. Just as a life lived on a landscape includes responding to the expected and unexpected rhythms of continuity and change, so too this research involved dynamic and nuanced work in order to accommodate what I was prepared and unprepared to encounter and make sense of.

Keeping the principles of dialogue and narrative in focus, there were three key questions that guided the field work:

1. What stories do participants tell about the development of this project?
2. What stories do participants tell about addressing mandates and needs?
3. And, what do participants seem to learn from each other as they exchange stories during their conversations?

The Bureaucracy of In-home Early Child Care in Southwest State

Efforts to regulate kith and kin providers, and the in-home care they offer, became an official priority just after the turn of the twenty-first century. A more precise focus on issues of quality and professionalization was brought forward at that time by CYFD administrator, Marisol Gonzalez: she recommended the creation of the Home Provider Initiative (HPI) as a means for systemic change. The aim was to reach out to all licensed and registered[3] child care providers across the state and improve the quality of care they offered in their homes, particularly through Head Start collaboration[4]. In January 2001, Gonzalez convened a workgroup[5] and asked members to design a state-wide training model through which the quality of registered in-home family child care providers' services and situations would be improved.

The HPI workgroup began by reviewing popular kith and kin issues[6], such as (1) the challenges of regulating social policy relative to diverse family values and privacy rights, (2) bureaucratizing family child care practices, (3) streamlining finance and accounting strategies, and (4) coordinating family child care with other early care programs (e.g., Even Start, Head Start) and collaborative efforts (e.g., YWCA, United Way/Success By 6). Using these as guideposts, the group determined priorities for Southwest State, proposed corollary goals and explored possibilities for achieving desired changes in the quality of in-home child care services. Four assumptions framed the subsequent logic for developing the training model. These included[7]

- The number of in-home family child care providers in Southwest State is increasing commensurate with the growth of the state's Hispanic/Latino popu-

lation—25% of the 8,400 registered providers reside in Dolores County alone, which is not surprising given its close proximity to El Brinco and Ciudad Juantá on the US-Mexico border—and as the Mexican heritage populations of other counties increase so do the number of registered in-home child care providers in each;
- Family child care homes are systems, although miniature by comparison, and these differ according to the provider; the larger the number of systems, the greater the chance of variation in the quality of child care;
- In contrast to child care centers, which typically operate from a point of view of service as profession, in-home child care providers engage their work more as a responsibility to the family or tradition, rather than as a professional career path; and, they tend to work in isolation from one another and other professionals; and,
- The difference in quality of in-home child care situations is not clearly established; however, any attempt to address quality differences must be developed within the sociocultural context of the providers themselves and the children and families they serve.

Meeting regularly from then on through December, 2001, members of the HPI workgroup outlined the basic program components. These generally included assessment, training, regulation, review and reimbursement, and technical assistance.

After a politically induced hiatus, related to the 2002 gubernatorial elections, CYFD's Office of Child Development (OCD) staff reconvened the workgroup to move forward on developing the HPI. In March 2003, the group began paying particular attention to the development of the training program component, which in its first iteration was referred to as the *16-hour Course*. The name reflected the proposed sixteen clock hours of actual instruction for participants. At that time, participants for the training course would be made up of registered in-home providers involved in both professional development and other state programming. Perhaps this was a reflection on the difficulties in locating non-participating providers who were willing to spend time in the pilot trial, as well as the ease of identifying those providers with formally established relationships with coordinators and other representatives of state organizations and programs. It remains unclear how the group came to this decision since remnant notes from the meeting do not specify a reason. The record simply reveals the change in plan. The March agenda further called for deliberations on the content for the course and listed pressing questions regarding dissemination, evaluation and action steps that would set in motion the implementation of the pilot test.

Two months later, Marisol Gonzalez called another meeting of the work group in order to review ideas for designing the training course. Prior to the meeting, Gonzalez put forward her perspective on the purpose of this initiative by suggesting in a memorandum that participants needed to understand that "[they]'ve raised [their] own children or seen how the family has raised children across the years and people have been okay…" but "[w]hat we now know children need may be beyond what we've done in our families." She emphasized that trainers for the course should communicate to participants that they must "…be open to going beyond or doing something differently than what [they had] done in the past." She further asserted that it would be important to gauge how participants "think about kids" in order for trainers to know how to explain their overarching "…philosophy of [how to treat] children and…raise them." And, she listed a series of ideas and issues that she supposed would become key curricular focuses for the training course:

1. Medical care—going to the dentist and doctor, using home remedies, making rituals of the five most important sanitary practices (i.e., washing hands, eating balanced meals, daily exercise, regular check-ups, and following directions for consuming medicines), and their rights with medical decisions;
2. Family issues—preventing participation in a gang, helping school age children pick proper affiliations, stating expectations and setting limits with family members, scripting family roles, corporal punishment, and discerning dynamics of abuse and neglect;
3. School readiness—social (i.e., getting along with others), emotional (i.e., self-regulation), physical (i.e., sitting still, and gross and fine motor coordination), cognitive (i.e., knowing the ABCs, counting, and following directions), and spiritual (i.e., making sure the child is never alone) development;
4. Community resources—access to library, church, and Medicaid; and,
5. Cultural issues—bilingualism, biculturalism, when the language (or dialect) at home is different than at school, use of birth names and nicknames.

Further, Gonzalez's notes in the memorandum made reference to a sense of urgency to ask course participants "Why do [they] take care of children?" She cast doubt on ideas such as "…keeping traditions alive" and "…leaving a legacy to children" as reasons for providing family child care. She suggested that this new training course should re-direct family providers' attention "…to what children need and how families can … access it." It is also important to highlight that, at the same time, she advised the use of Mexican-heritage dichos, or Spanish words of wisdom, such as "bien educado" (i.e., someone who is well mannered, respectful and smart whether or not he or she has attended school) or "dime con quien andas y te diré quien eres," (i.e., tell me with whom you spend your time and I'll tell you who you are) to draw participants' attention to the ideas to be presented in the course curriculum.

A final point for discussion was the configuration of the curriculum across the sixteen clock hours. Gonzalez recommended the group segment the training into hour-long blocks, according to "big ideas" they would identify as those most relevant to "the needs of providers." A specific big idea, or curricular topic, would then be highlighted for each hour of instruction, with no more than three to five main points used to teach that topic[8]. She included a precursor outline that clustered certain ideas and issues, to be addressed as key curricular topics of the 16-hour course, into nine categories: (1) health and safety; (2) family business; (3) ages and stages of child development; (4) literacy and numeracy; (5) positive, appropriate discipline; (6) parent and provider interaction; (7) healthy children; (8) mental health; and, (9) community resources.

Development of the 16-hour Course

The actual contract for developing the 16-hour Course was awarded in January 2004. Close collaboration with representatives of related agencies (e.g., Family Services Division staff of the OCD of CYFD, Head Start) was required so that the curriculum and materials would be consistent with other initiatives promoted by CYFD.

This new course was based on the model of the 45-hour course with explicit emphases on child development, language development, social and emotional development, health, guidance, literacy and numeracy, the learning environment, and family relations/family support. Concerns and issues of participants, moreover, could be included as additional curricular topics. The 16 clock hours were to be divided into eight, two-hour modules. These time bound blocks were supposed to serve as the organizing structure for course content, as well as an accommodating opportunity for providers to either take these concurrently—for the purpose of acquiring licensure—or individually—as "stand alone" units of professional development for maintaining their current registered status. Specific course content would be outlined and sequenced in the form of a Facilitator/Trainer manual; and, packets—written at a basic readability level of *third to sixth grade* in both Spanish and English—were to be included as a reference for participants. Within the scope of the course content outline, and reference materials, facilitators/trainers were encouraged to recognize the cultural orientation, values, mores and traditions of all participants involved in the training course. Making reference to the Mexican heritage notion of *charlar*, training was meant to include informal discussions, or conversations, in order to engage participants. And, eventually the course was referred to as Charlas.

A budget of $19,005.00 was allocated to support this work. A sum of $1500.00 was devoted to the acquisition of curricular materials (e.g., pamphlets, books, toys, videos, etc.), and $3200.00 was marked for soliciting the assistance of community-identified experts as contributing authors and translators. To allow for meeting the expectation of close collaboration, $350.00 was allotted for travel. The remainder was devoted to providing stipends for the principal investigators and paying fringe benefit costs and administrative overhead levies.

New directions: From 16 to 18 hours

Nicole Bush and Lázaro Reales, Southwest State University (SWSU) faculty and co-directors of the project funded to develop the professional development initiative, were aware from the start that they had to consider several immitigable conditions:

- In-home family child care providers often begin their work day as early as six o'clock in the morning, and they may care for children until seven or eight o'clock at night;
- they, consequently, have limited periods of time to devote to their own individual and family needs;

- the clear majority have never participated in comprehensive training opportunities focused on current policies, practices or professionalism for in-home family care provision;
- several are monolingual Spanish speakers, and a majority are Spanish-English bilinguals, who either have legitimate concerns about how to make sure that English-only speakers understand them and/or that they themselves accurately understand English-only speakers; and,
- many face literacy challenges on a daily basis, such as being unfamiliar with formal protocols for requesting social services, struggling to read legal documents or complete institutional forms, and feeling awkward about participating openly in public forums or meetings.

It was important to Bush and Reales that state officials keep clearly in mind that Southwest State's in-home family child care providers are predominantly Latina and indigenous heritage women. They vary in age from the late twenties to seventy years or more, Furthermore, they contend with multiple competing demands, regulated by the constraints of a mostly unyielding schedule, on a daily basis. As Bush and Reales explained "...many of these individuals are grandmothers, grandfathers, mothers, fathers, aunts, uncles, step-parents and/or guardians...." Given these complexities, it was critical to see this as a challenge of working with family members who work in diverse situations—whether in their own families or with other families—rather than seeing this as training a mass of sales personnel who work in uniform for a large company.

Their first step toward course development was to elaborate the curricular design for the training course. Although eight, two-hour, sessions had been delineated by the CYFD contract, Bush and Reales began by considering whether or not "everything these providers needed" could be addressed in the 16-hour time frame. Reflecting on previous work developing other courses, it occurred to them that "the average person who...[participated in similar courses]...[did not] need to know as much about the business aspect, whereas in-home child care providers [did]." This was confirmed by talking further with colleagues, both academic and practitioners in the field. Eventually, in conversations with Jana Cole, Coordinator of SWSU's La Visión Institute, they talked at length about how they "...really need[ed] to help [in-home providers] think of what [they were] doing as a business, and see themselves more as professionals." And, Nicole Bush recalled that,

> "Jerilee Loya had been conducting training ... on Dollars and Sense, and [she pointed out] there was a well-developed training program for center people, but there wasn't an equivalent for in-home providers. At most of the workshops the [in-home] providers themselves indicated they had no business knowledge about tax laws, enforcement codes, contractual provisions, etc. They even expressed utter surprise in learning that they could enforce a contract. I think it was a mutual realization between the providers themselves and the people who did the training ...."

Bush and Reales then took into consideration that in-home providers feel frustration with patrons who either do not pay, fail to pay in a timely manner, or breach scheduling agreements over and over. Thus, they drew the conclusion that there was a void in the proposed design: There was no explicit requirement to address business policies and practices. Most, if not all, of the providers who would participate in that course, would not refer to themselves as business people. Even though they set their working hours for care provision, and charged a nominal fee, they explained their service as an act of commitment to, or love for, children and family. Moreover, they rarely established contracts with kith or kin, imposed consequences in the face of failure to pay a pledged fee, or enforced scheduling limits. In addition to addressing these matters, Bush and Reales were intent on making sure that in-home family child care providers would be able to avoid unnecessary tax problems, which had become progressively pervasive over time.

So, the business module developed as a latent realization. Through recurring conversations about whom the audience would be, as well as what the difference was between this population and that of participants taking other courses, Bush and Reales decided that another two-hour module was needed to accommodate the additional content, as well as allow time for conversation. They conjectured that it would be appropriate for all in-home child care providers, not just kith and kin providers. CYFD officials agreed that these revisions were appropriate. As a result, the 16-hour kith and kin course, *Charlas*, became an 18-hour in-home family child care providers' course.

The course name reflected first a recognition of recent research implications— that didactic efforts to train family child care providers in a standardized fashion are much less likely to be successful than an approach that emerges out of participatory discussions which look like, and sound like, *natural conversations*. Second, the curriculum design signals the intention to ensure that every trainer would be *on the same page* and use *conversation* in their facilitation of the course. According to their conceptual framework, the facilitator, a family child care specialist, would reserve as much time as possible for participants to talk through their concerns, confusions, insights and lasting questions. With these key hypotheses in mind, Bush and Reales worked closely with Jerilee Loya to articulate the pedagogical practices for delivering each training module.

The specifics of the course curriculum were outlined by teams. Bush, Reales and Loya formed a leadership team, with each taking on responsibility for forming a working group, comprised of well-known and respected community members who were also experienced early child care providers. These consultants assisted in drafting one or more of the nine training modules.

They met approximately once every two or three weeks in a six week interim period between the contract award and the first training session to share accomplishments, such as articulation of essential questions for conversations related to CYFD competencies, structure and timing of activities, related materials and readings. Drafts were also shared over the interim period. In the end, Nicole Bush edited the penultimate drafts and prepared the final course guidebook.

In writing the course curriculum, they found themselves deliberating extensively on the challenging question of the place of conventional reading and writing. They recalled that they were cautious because they recognized the differences in participants' literacy experiences and formal literacy education, as well as felt an obligation to the prevailing public expectation that professionals demonstrate control of the conventions of standard English. Given this acumen, and the CYFD expectation, and directive, of selecting materials written at an *eighth grade* level, they felt a strong sense of conflict as they made their final determination about how much and what kinds of reading and writing should be integral to the curriculum and pedagogy for the course. This was intensified once the pilot sessions had been conducted. More specifically, Bush remembered that most of the participants in the pilot course believed it would have been easier if they had been able to just talk to the facilitators about their evaluation of the course rather than trying to write their comments. They suggested, in fact, that the facilitators write for them. This was, clearly, a disquieting issue to resolve.

In final preparation for the pilot trials, a SWSU graduate student translated the written lesson plans for each module. As Bush recalled, "...that became an issue too. Southwest Mexican Spanish isn't Mexican Spanish, and we had extensive discussions about the [different] meanings of individual words and ... phrasing of ideas.... One of the things we realized from other courses was that we had to be linguistically responsive, ..." Materials were then collected and catalogued for each module respectively. There were considerably more English print materials assembled for every module: Spanish print materials were included in only two modules.

In May 2004, Bush and Reales had completed the 18-hour course curriculum handbook for facilitators. It included a welcome letter to facilitators, a rationale for the Charlas course, an overview of course design and goals, an outline of key facilitation principles, and a lesson plan for each of the nine modules (e.g., see Figure 1.1 below).

Figure 1.1—Summary example of *Families and Communities* (Module 1).

The lesson plan includes conversation pieces, learning goals, resources and facilitation narrative.

One learning goal for the first module is that participants will have "described families and family systems," referring to the introductory material of the chapter that lists the ways that people create and/or are born into multi-layered families (p. 3). The guide lists various ways in which families are enacted across the landscapes of faith, sexuality, language traditions, marriage, divorce, gender (and gender roles), and communities. The first activity invites participants to share something about her/his family. Another expanding activity centers on discussing the *family system*, likening the interdependence of family members to the functioning of a car, and listing stages of family development.

Finally, there is attention to communication between family members, family childcare providers, and the children in their care. The expanding activity in this section focuses on using *I-messages* instead of *You-messages* as one method of minimizing language that can be construed as "blaming, judging, or evaluating." (Nicole Bush, 2004, p. 9)

Conversation Pieces:
Families have different members, roles, values, beliefs, traditions, languages, and cultures;

Many factors add stress to families' lives; and,

There are community resources for families who find themselves at high levels of stress, in conflict, with medical and/or emotional challenges, or lacking resources to meet their basic needs (e.g., food and shelter).

Resources:
1. Newsprint, tape and markers;
2. Blocks;
3. Handouts—
    a. What is a family?
    b. Family systems
    c. Child care provider Bill of Rights
    d. Communication Skills
    e. Influences on Families
    f. Synthesizing Activity; and,
4. Local community resources.

Lesson plans were designed to direct a facilitator's attention to *conversation pieces*, *learning goals*, and an outline of *material resources* in order to promote action and meaningful discussion. Immediately following, a scope and sequence for addressing the module's topic was narrated in terms of what a facilitator might say to introduce the module, start a conversation, prompt participants into an activity and continue the conversation with a sharper focus on the learning goals. Each narrative was structured according to guiding questions (e.g., What is a family? Why is it important for children to select activities? What are the necessary city and state requirements for a, in-home family child care business? Or, what are the language abilities of young children from birth to age eight in the context of family and culture?), with specific suggestions for expanded activities, and finally a relevant synthesizing activity aimed at assessing what participants found meaningful and useful. Facilitators were not expected to follow the plans as scripts; instead they were encouraged to use these design features as general reference points for completing the two-hour module

The pilot test of Charlas

The next step in the process was to recruit participants for the pilot test of the 18-hour course. Nicole Bush and Lázaro Reales worked with SWSU La Visión Institute staff to recruit participants and identify two locations for pilot testing in Dolores County: Veranera and Las Golondrinas. Spanish was the language of instruction for the course in Chaparral; and, English was the primary language of instruction for the course in Las Golondrinas. Teams of two or three facilitators worked together to run each training session. In addition, the use of the facilitators' guidebook, children's books, games and toy kits were distributed to all pilot participants who completed the nine modules. Bush emphasized that this encouraged "…collaborative reflection afterwards which helped [the teams] come to important impressions, insights and interests…," and meaningful feedback to further revise the course's curriculum and pedagogy.

The Veranera pilot was conducted with 17 predominantly Spanish-speaking in-home family child care providers, and as Bush pointed out, many of whom "…were grandparents…[t]hey were [also] relatives, because two husbands and wives took the course, and all of the others were mothers and sisters, [even] a mother and two of her daughters…took the course." Lázaro Reales collaborated with other Institute staff to run this pilot. In retrospect, Reales offered that "…it was a very interesting time, I really enjoyed it. I thought the intersection between the Veranera context and the modules themselves, the conflict that had happened…, especially in the area of business practices…[t]here was so much resistance to that…from the participants …." One colleague remembered that "[they] do this because [they] *love* [their] kids, and this is familia and all this kind of stuff." She explained that "[t]hese kinds of responses were very telling to me." And, she further emphasized that "…what I really learned from that is that … we really have to rethink how we would introduce that business module to families [in Veranera]. …in family [child] care, these Latinas, and Latinos, had *big* problems with that." She concluded by suggesting that "… the other thing about the curriculum is that we really wanted to look at the idea of care—which I don't know if we did—I haven't reflected [enough] on it, and we really wanted to present the idea of caring for young children versus educating kids, and *now* how it's fitting into the larger picture, which it's very evident that it's part of this getting children ready for school.…"

In thinking about the significance of conversation to the course, it occurred to them that a facilitators' training course would have to be developed, because the family care provider course could not be implemented as conversations if the facilitator did not understand such a process. And, they realized that they couldn't assume that everyone who would eventually facilitate the 18 hour course would have had the kind of education and experience required for constructing this kind of an approach to adult learning. A three-hour facilitator training course was therefore created; again, its conceptualization involved a combination of La Visión staff and experienced family child care professionals from the Las Golondrinas community so that diverse perspectives would inform the assessment of the quality of the course, as well as guide the future teaching of this course. In between the completion of this pilot and the start of the Las Golondrinas trial run, Nicole Bush and Lázaro Reales arranged for a training session to take place, with an aim to prepare a team of facilitators to meet the imminent demand for delivering the course as they had conceptualized it. According to Jerilee Loya, the entire child care specialist staff at La Visión Institute, and Carla Arduino, representing the OCD, took part in that training session. The following day the Las Golondrinas pilot was conducted.

An equivalent number of providers, a group of women only, some of whom were Spanish-English bilinguals who cared for their own family's, as well as neighbors' children, participated in the Las Golondrinas pilot session. One of the facilitators described the subsequent pilot effort as one with an "… approach, where it's interactive. It's not an adult *teaching* an adult, it's an adult sharing, empowering, an adult. And the way it works…is you declare what you know. You get the people to talk about what they know, about everything and anything, depending on the topic, of course." For example, she recounted that facilitators tried to encourage conversation by prompting: "'Tell me about your grandchild? How does he think? What things can he do? And, you know, you just have a conversation with a person…and they would tell you about their grandchild, but they don't know the way we see it as educators." She continued "…we let them declare what they know. Then, we'll talk about th[at], and … interact with them through activities, through videos, with brainstorming, through idea sharing. [T]hen, we'll support it with documents, with brochures. [A]t the end of the two hours they mesh what they know with what we've taught them, and it's called synthesizing what you know. … The way we do it, because these are relatives, … we have like a closure conversation session; in other words, somebody would document, but everybody gives their idea, but maybe the instructor or group leader would document what they were saying." Bush attended a few of the modular sessions at the Las Golondrinas pilot to remain connected with the process. Bush and Reales subsequently debriefed with facilitators immediately after the course ended in order to clarify any confusions and identify what revisions needed to be made before submitting a final copy of the Facilitator Guidebook to CYFD staff for their evaluation and final approval.

Once the revisions were accommodated into the course design, on-going implementation of the course for other in-home family care providers all across Dolores County was launched. Jerilee Loya hired two Family Childcare Specialists to be responsible for recruiting participants and implementing this course in La Visión's service area.

According to the feedback from participants in both pilot courses, the most salient outcome was that before the course they had felt completely alone in their work, however, through the course they bonded with one another as both professionals and friends. Many of the participants in the Las Golondrinas pilot group remarked that they "…would love to find a way to continue meeting as a group…"

and discussing their needs and questions, as well as being a community again." One participant said that as a result of the Charlas experience "[she] found the confidence in [herself] to go to college." She has recently been attending Dolores Branch Community College of SWSU to complete courses for an Early Childhood Education license. Several of her peers requested that La Visión Institute offer additional courses for in-home family care providers[9].

For many, if not most, it was a profoundly meaningful—they began to look to each other as brokers, confidents, learners, and teachers. As Bush further explained, they felt "... a sense of affirmation, even empowerment, that they had been recognized as esteemed individuals and bona fide professionals. The expressions on their faces seemed to suggest a delight much like that reflected by a child who receives the birthday present she has been solemnly wishing for in her dreams." There were several cases of mother-daughter, or sister-sister, pairs who completed the training course together. Even these cases, both parties talked about the new kind of relationship formed between them because of the extent and nature of dialogue they experienced. It gave Bush and Reales pause that although family childcare providers are an incredibly diverse group, they have similar needs for collegiality and friendship. "Because they are isolated," Bush pointed out, "including relatives who share this professional experience, they are deeply appreciative of this kind of an opportunity...."

Reminiscing about the process, bush suggested "... we [were working with] a neglected population of childcare providers ... typically there's a childcare food conference during the year, which they attend [and] receive credits to maintain their eligibility status ... but, other than that, because of their isolation, they just don't feel supported." And, she acknowledged that several issues remained priorities, including: opening up access for in-home family care providers to financial and institutional resources, addressing disconnections between grandparents and parents related to daily priorities and family aspirations, understanding the shift between yesterday and today in educational expectations, providing opportunities for improving providers' literacy levels (i.e., reading and writing in both Spanish and English), and securing counseling and career advisory services. "Because I feel that family childcare providers are in many ways the backbone of the childcare profession," she concluded, "we can't neglect them.... Not only in Southwest State, but all over the country, the majority of children are in family childcare...."

Realizing and Addressing Different Needs

So, what stories are told about addressing needs? And, what can be learned from these stories about working for in-home childcare? These questions were explored in terms of what might be learned about working with diverse providers, with different needs, and respectively the families and children they work with, in order to promote meaningful training for other family child care specialists. These were also examined to consider relevant implications for such intricate and important initiatives in the future.

First, attention is given to developing conceptual, conversational and cultural competence in course facilitators in order to realize and address the needs of participants. Next the focus is on participants' call for relevant learning, in terms of their particular situations and understandings. Further, the unanimous sense of learning *in* community is discussed as important evidence of attention to their needs. And, the manners in which the two Family Child Care Specialists facilitated the pilot 18-hour courses, listening sensitively and seriously to the providers input, follows as evidence of addressing what families and their children needed and wanted.

The need for conceptual, conversational and cultural competence

Those involved in the project, irrespective of their position or role, storied their understandings of the Charlas experience: these stories referred to the experience as something that had indeed happened during the course, but also as what would be brought forward with them beyond the course. The experience seemed to be situated in an on-going dialogue that began with the 18-clock hours of Charlas and then reached beyond the temporal boundaries of the course schedule into their relationships with each other and work with families and children. So, what was "found" through this particular analytic-interpretive approach, is re-presented as narrative, because this genre points to the continuously interactive and situated nature of things. In terms of finding answers to the original research questions, the findings have been textured as narrative tensions that must be faced over and over in order to consider, let alone meet, needs.

Although approval for the training course and funding for a pilot run had been achieved, there remained certain challenges. Recorded as a set of notes, that apparently emerged from the developers' own fortuitous conversations that took place in unanticipated spaces and at unusual times, and actually referred to as talk from "the parking lot," these annotations centered on the challenges of dealing with the language, literacy and cultural diversity of different providers and the professional competence of potential facilitators. It was then, for example, important to the course designers consider to figure out how to address variations in the providers' expression and practice of English and/or Spanish literacy. And, it mattered to them that they determine strategic ways to recruit facilitator candidates who were Spanish-English bilingual, had previous experience with teaching adults, and conveyed confidence in addressing complicated issues, such as abuse, neglect, custody disputes, and immigration. As a way to pay on-going attention to these challenges, a rubric of goals, outcomes, procedures and timelines was delineated and distributed[10].

As expected, the pilot implementation took place in different locations (i.e., Alomogordo, Chaparral, and Las Golondrinas), over a fifteen month period. Approximately 200 in-home family child care providers participated in the pilot sessions of Charlas, one third of which were offered in Spanish (see Figures 1.2, 1.3 and 1.4 below for an explicit summary of these indicators).

Figure 1.2. Summary of number of English training sessions in Alajuela, co-facilitated by Victoria and a peer, by date, including number of participants.

Dates	# of participants
February 3 – April 1, 2004	11
April 3 – May 1, 2004	8
May 4 – June 29, 2004	8
August 3 – 31, 2004	4
September 11 – October 2, 2004	20**
October 4 – 27, 2004	9
November 6 – 20, 2004	12
December 1 – 9, 2004	7
TOTAL	79

Figure 1.3. Summary of number of Spanish training sessions in Churrialba by date, including number of participants.

Dates	# of participants
January 3 – 15, 2005	17
February 1- 12, 2005	18**
March 2 – 30, 2005	10
April 11 – 23, 2005	11
May 2 – 19, 2005	5
TOTAL	61

Figure 1.4. Summary of number of English training sessions in Las Colimas by date, including number of participants.

Dates	# of participants
January 3 – February 6, 2005	10
February 12 – 25, 2005	10
March 1 – April 5, 2005	10
April 9 – 26, 2005	9
May 2 – 25, 2005	6
TOTAL	45

To approach their work in a dialogic fashion, as well as assess the success of their work (i.e., clarify from an internal point of view as to how the course was relevant to the needs of providers), the facilitators used two methods of formative evaluation. The first was a pre-post differentiation measure, which took the form of a nine-item questionnaire, with one of each item representing the nine modules. The scale of responses ascended in the following order: "I have never heard about this topic…," "I have heard about this topic; however, …," "I have some idea, but …," "I have a clear idea…,". Then, the facilitators handed out, almost always at the end of a module session, a standardized short-answer questionnaire that served as both a synthesizing activity for the participants and a teaching evaluation for the facilitators. The three questions of this measure asked: "What did you learn today?" "Why was it important to talk about [the module topic]?" And, "What will you do to learn more about this topic?" Nearly every participant completed these forms, noting specific ideas they had discussed during the course modules. For the most part, these measures illustrated participants' capsule reiterations of topic objectives (e.g., children are unique and special and we have to treat them with respect), which were completely consistent with those outlined for the course curriculum.

A much stronger, and more visceral, sense of what participants reasoned as valid and significant for addressing their needs, however, was directly apparent in their in-class interactions and their reflective journaling. Therefore, the discussion now turns to the narrative re-presentation of what they made obvious in their immediate conversations and pointed out in their post-course reflections.

The need for relevant learning

Having opportunities to talk about what was mandated by state policy and program requirements, their unique situations, as well as their desire to continue providing excellent care for children, were cited over and over as what made the time spent in the 18-hour course worth their while. Their reflections revealed that these were especially valued because, from their point of view, their immediate needs were recognized as priorities. In their post workshop journaling, for example, they talked about *being able* to ask their own questions about health and safety issues and discuss problems they faced because of contradictory policy pronouncements. They referred to these situations as occurring both within a modular session and across all modules. Perhaps these opportunities were so deeply regarded because these were openly and explicitly addressed, unlike any of their previous professionalizing experiences? Or, perhaps, the value lies in the particular ways they were addressed by the family child care specialists, who facilitated the workshop and encouraged them to open up such learning opportunities?

In reading across participant journalings, their scrupulous sense of satisfaction in having "learn[ed] more" was preponderant. Two women, each with a number of years of experience as family child care providers, suggested that in the 18-hour course they found multiple opportunities to gain access to previously untold information. One reflected, "A mí sí, me sirvió mucho las clases, porque aprendí muchas cosas que no sabía…, y muchas gracias que nos orienta para saber más." Her colleague continued, "En este programa que estamos, aprendí mucho más que las séis horas que vamos…, lo que digo es que nosotros hemos ido a las clases de las 6 horas, nunca nos había explicado eso, nos enseñan a hacer juegitos, y todo eso, … [pero] no hay nada de información." (Participant Journaling, March 30, 2005) Further, they explained that the experience was so different and meaningful because the course occurred over time. Participants pointed out that "[c]ada clase uno se aprenda cosas nuevas, y más…," (Participant Journaling, March 30, 2005), and "I mean it's so full of information that I really, really, [raises voice] *can't stress it enough*,…" Participant Journaling, October 29, 2004) Comments such as these suggest that the course not only focused on information and issues that were immediately meaningful to the participants, but also provided relevance beyond an ordinary presentation. It advocated for them to consider and discuss information and issues as professionals indeed would. Again, it is not difficult to understand why most, if not all, were able to sustain their interest in and their willingness to attend the entire course, night after night—which was considerably longer than any other they had taken—while still working full time.

These opportunities cleared the path for talking about confusing issues, learning accurate, or even new, information about state policy and appropriate practice, and asking troubling questions. "It opened my eyes a lot more. I don't care how much it costs! $30, $40, $50. I would take the class again!" (Participant Journaling, February 26, 2005) Appraisals such as this were offered frequently, principally in regards to learning about child development, health and safety issues, paying taxes, and meeting the terms of food program subsidy requirements—all of which were explicitly discussed in the respective modules' curriculum and reiterated throughout the remainder of the course. Two participants articulated their praise for the facilitator's attention to questions about child behavior and development in this way: "'The child development and learning was really a nice module..., knowing about child development does help caregivers develop realistic expectations for children's behaviors, and that is so important, [turning to address another participant], right, don't you agree?' 'Yes, yes I do, because each child grows and develops in his or her own special way'." (Participant Journaling, October 29, 2004) Other participants juxtaposed their frustration with the prevalence of misinformation among their peers about, for example, *back pay* and *taxes*, and their relief in having access to learn accurate information. One emphasized how disconcerting it was to not be aware: "En el programa [food subsidy required 6-hour annual trainings] no se explica que tiene que pagar taxes aquí, tiene que pagar taxes allá... uno va a firmar contrato; atrás del contrato, no dice nada de eso. ...". (Participant Journaling, March 30, 2005) Another explained adamantly, "Eso de backpay, también yo no sabía que hacen backpay...". (Participant Journaling, March 30, 2005) And, in regards to requirements for the food program, three participants exclaimed consecutively: "I was told it was mandatory;" "I was told it was soon to be mandatory;" and, "I was told that it was mandatory after February 1st"." Allowing for further comments and queries, the facilitator then asked: "Does everyone know about childcare subsidy? The food program?" Given the mix of responses, and the obvious contradictions in information, she spent considerable time not only explaining the program, policy statutes and procedures for accessing this relevant information but also repeatedly confirming individual petitions for confirmation. (Observation Notes, January 20, 2005)

Participants also offered explanations of how they were challenged and encouraged to consider their questions through the on-going conversations, or dialogue, of the class, "So [elongated], when we work together, especially with these classes that are really great with information, the behaviors, the feelings, the language development, to see what phases they're in, what stages they're in, [we learn] so that we may inform the parents." (Participant Journaling, October 29, 2004) Another suggested that, "estas 18 horas [sirven] para poder seguir cuidar a niños..., cada clase uno se aprenda cosas nuevas." And, the opportunity to consider the awkward question of how to address troubling issues—such as (non)payment, by family or friends, for child care—was equally noted. One, in particular, reflected: "I was taking care of this little girl, and [her mother always said] 'I'll pay you next week.' I didn't want to tell her anything because I was friends with her mom, but my daughter kept telling me, 'Mom, it's like your job! Who cares if they get mad'?" Through ensuing conversation among her peers, and with the facilitator, she was able to determine for herself an approach to discussing the issue with her friend. Clearly, these participants reflected that by and large they found the 18-hour course relevant to their interests in becoming more knowledgable professionals, communicating necessary information to parents and understanding new ways to provide care and support for children.

It is not difficult, then, to see that these family child care providers are pointing out their appreciation for opportunities to have access to accurate information about policy requirements, realize their rights as business-professionals, as well as learn how to navigate between these and ask for assistance. Their evaluations, moreover, denote strong agreement that the course was meeting their needs. Many agreed with the recommendation that "[t]he parents *should* take this class too. Oh, definitely! Yeah, parents." (Participant Journaling, October 29, 2005)

The need for a sense of community

A sense of learning *in community* was underscored by providers as the most important way in which their needs were being met. It mattered to them because, from their point of view, it meant that their concerns and experiences were real. In the words of one participant, and affirmed by a chorus of her peers, there was no clear distinction between learning and being in a community. She saw the process of being together, in the ways the facilitators encouraged them and they reached out to each other, as vital to the opportunity to learn and clarify their perspective on who they were as individuals and a group of professionals: "A mí me gustó convivir con mis compañeras, las aplicaciones que nos dió [la maestra] pos, me dió gusto saber de que somos [otras toman parte] proveedoras, de que nos engañen muy fácil..., y saber [ahora] como podemos defendernos...". (Participant Journaling, March 30, 2005) Several participants explained the significance of community in terms of small class size, suggesting it as a quality that engendered a comfortable and manageable learning situation. "The 6 hours go so fast. It's worth it, but it doesn't help you a lot. [In this class] the community opens! [Here we have] smaller groups." Another highlighted the contrast in the conditions between this experience and previous mandatory ones by declaring, "Sí, es más importante, esta 18, que las seís horas." Another further substantiated, "¡...y esta es porque aquí somos un grupo pequeño y allí somos cantidad!" (Participant Journaling, March 30, 2005)

Similarly, the facilitators perceived a sense of community to be unmistakably important to participants. They contended this had something to do with the small size of each class, but also with a focus on real conversation. They also reflected on their work regularly through their own reflective journaling exercise, which included examining their concerns, questions and lingering impressions. Following the completion of the third implementation of the 18-hour course, they talked about the intimacy nurtured and protected in the ways they tried to relate to the participants and the participants tried to relate to them. There were a number of examples, from across the different sessions they each facilitated, evident in their reflective talk; however, there was one, in particular, that served as a touchstone. It seemed to call them to remember more vividly the care, trust, and vulnerability created through this work of using real conversations to learn. In the most recent Health and Safety module, one provider shared a true story about addressing the issue of child sexual abuse. She looked, hesitantly but hopefully, to the relationships she and her peers had established in order to open up a new opportunity to learn:

> V: First we talked about physical..., looking for different things..., children..., we talked about personal responsibility..., [and then] I went into child abuse..., in the Health and Safety, there's a portion on child abuse—that's where we got into it ...;
> C: We were talking about this, and she brought up..., [long pause], one of the kids that she watches was sexually abused, and I think that's where everybody started to be...;
> V: ...conscientious...;
> C: She's the one who found out [about the abuse] and from then, I think little by little, they seemed a little bit closer...;
> V: ...and I actually, what I could pick up, I would say that there were maybe other providers who that had happened to...;
> C: ...and they [the participants] acted like they knew each other...;
> V: That was what I found almost astonishing, because there seemed..., she didn't feel comfortable enough to share, but she knew about the impact that it [sexual abuse] had had in her life, whether it was herself, or somebody else..., we had eight, and I would say about maybe three [who also mentioned the issue with personal references], a high percentage...;
> M: One of them said, [in the journaling I did with participants] "We've had similar things in our lives and we didn't share, but you're helping us...;"
> V: Two came out, and you figure, look at the percentages of the women who were in there..., one of them had gone to therapy, one of them had discussed it with her mother...; [and,]
> C: ...and that's just the ones we know about, who had experience with abuse..., how many others? ...and, I think this room is a very intimate room..., the group is small, the numbers are just right..., the conversations are more intimate.[11]

Other women responded to her disclosure by revealing that they had had like experiences: "We've had similar things in our lives and we didn't share, but you're [to participants and facilitators] helping us." (Observation Notes, December 9, 2004) Their words allude to deeply personal benefits experienced through this specific critical conversation, as well as those that preceded it and the others that followed in the 18-hour course. Creating community and communion in conversation appeared to help them connect lingering feelings and memories of past experiences to new ways to address similar issues today as they strive to provide safe care. Again and again, participants proclaimed the need for this kind of public sharing because they do not find such support in other places or professional venues.

The fact that they shared such vulnerability, at such a relatively early point in time in the course, is an indication of the promise of the facilitators' manner and practices, as well as conversation as a conduit to realize relevant but difficult issues. More than ever, it is a signal for the need to continue creating this kind of communal practice—an experience in which individuals indeed see each other as members of a community and support each other. Again, from the facilitators' point of view, this particular form of sharing fostered a more conscientious attitude among the participants around the complexities of various issues related to children's health, safety and well-being. The above exchange also exemplifies the ways in which the natural movements of conversation provide unforeseen, unexpected opportunities for more lucid exploration and examination of an issue or a question. In this case, one woman risked to share a personally relevant experience that was related to the curriculum at hand. Her sharing, and her peers' sensitive responses, opened up a space in which they all were able to consider the immediacy and urgency of this, and similar issues, in providing care for children.

Even when the curriculum was redundant, participants maintained that sharing their experiences and exploring each others' ways of knowing were personally satisfying and professionally rewarding: "Some of the stuff I already knew, but it's always good to have a meeting like this…," "See, people who have lived it, well, I've heard about it …. But, you have to live it, and listen to somebody else that has gone through it." (Participant Journaling, December 16, 2004)

Moreover, there was a nearly unanimous sense that the creation of community had something to do with the facilitator(s). Most participants noted in their reflective journaling that "lo más importante es la maestra, la maestra tiene mucha paciencia con nosotros…". (Participant Journaling, March 30, 2005). In the February course, all the participants decided to journal as a community and concurred, "…good teachers…, she's very good! …, they held my interest and my mind wanders real easily…, it depends on the teacher!" (Participant Journaling, February 26, 2005) Respect and validation were cited as expressions of the facilitators' manner toward and with them in the class sessions. Such respect was viewed as a matter of real conversation, including repeated sharing of experiences from beginning to end of the 18 hours. One participant explained in relational terms how the facilitators' dispositions specifically cultivated a needed sense of community: "I want to tell you, 'thank you,' for lifting our spirits…, we're doing our best as providers to children, [and] others look down on us…, and we provide to the best of our abilities…, thank you for that respect." (Participant Journaling, December 16, 2004)

The 18-hour course, engendered by the nature of real conversations and the facilitators' particular praxis, thus reflected the topography of a vibrant community. The realness of the conversations was textured by the participants' diverse voices and experiences, the expert perceptions and interpretations of the facilitators, and the curricular mandates of state policy. Nonetheless, the well-being of family childcare providers, and the well-being of the children in their care, were considered with intentional respect and seriousness.

The needs of families and children in their care[12]

Attention to the needs of families, and more specifically the children in their care, was central to the dialogic course of the conversations for every content module. Although the modules were most often introduced by their prescribed curriculum, careful attention to the kinds of comments and questions exchanged by facilitators and participants coupled with a propensity among all involved to elaborate meanings opened up dialogic turns, which then nurtured the gradual emergence of conversation. With each turn, the ways providers had addressed families' and their children's needs in the past, as well as how they would seek to do so in the future, were pondered. The two Family Child Care Specialists facilitating the pilot 18-hour courses used a variety of mediums—from asking direct questions and soliciting opinions to welcoming storytelling as well as prompting focused reflection—as means for turning the focus of the conversations on to what families and their children needed as well as wanted. Their exercise of these different methods was not always, in fact it seemed rarely, predetermined; instead, the turn to conversations seemed more intuitive. That is, it was unmistakably connected to both the facilitator's assessment of the emotional, intellectual, and political dynamics of the immediate discussion and her hope for carrying that beyond the apparent present understandings.

To illustrate the dialogic nature of this work, a narrative portrait of Victoria Cadena has been crafted from observation notes and her own journaling. This portrait features Victoria working with participants in a business practices module. Although brief, this portrays a vivid picture of the nature of her particular focus on the needs of families and children.

Victoria—
V: *We're going to go through this fairly quickly because this has been a long week.*
P1: *Mine isn't a business because I'm not working in a daycare, I just take care of my two grandchildren...,*
P2: *Te mandaron el W2?*
V: *Do you want to tell me about your experience with that process? [All of the participants begin discussing end of year gross tax receipts, and the benefits of all at once or once a year; then the mixed conversation wanes.]*
V: *How did you feel? What was your experience?*
P1: *I am just taking care of my grandchildren, and they don't pay me like a day care. [Acknowledging her response, nodding affirmatively, the facilitator then turns to the whiteboard and writes the question: Why are contracts necessary if I take care of my grandchildren?]*
P3: *Because otherwise they can get away with not paying you at all.*
P4: *It's something you can use to back yourself up with. You see, I was taking care of this little girl..., [her mother always said] "I'll pay you next week," but I didn't want to tell her anything because I was friends with her mom, but my daughter kept telling me, "Mom, it's like your job! Who cares if [she] get[s] mad?" [All of the participants continue the conversation, explaining the different expenses they incur as part of their daily work with young children; as the intensity wanes, more precise individual turn taking resumes.]*
P5: *I buy them school clothes, toys...,*
P6: *[With] all this grandma pays for, it adds up to my pay—gas and mileage. [In response to this turn in the focus, the facilitator hands out a Calendar Keeper and mentions that it includes Sundays, and has places to record all expenses, including a pocket for receipts. While she announces the different features and possible purposes of the Calendar Keeper, several women briefly discuss the food subsidy program.]*
P5: *I was told it was mandatory...,*
P4: *I was told it was soon to be mandatory...,*

P3: *I was told that it was mandatory after February 1st. [P3 explains that she prepares taxes, and several other participants begin to ask her questions about regulations and their particular circumstances.]*
P6: *Do I have to pay taxes if I make under $2,000 a year?*
P3: *I take care of 6 kids, so I make more than $8,000, so it's better for me to file taxes...,*
P2: *Federal le quita y el estado le da para pagar [los impuestos] federales...,*
P3: *I've prepared taxes for elderly and received home grown vegetables as payment...,*
P7: *God will bless you.*
P3: *If they don't have your social [security number], they don't know that you get your money; and, if the parent claims you on their tax form, the state has your information.*
P8: *My daughter gets a lump sum; but, she didn't tell me...,*
P9: *That's kids for you..., [Everyone in the room laughs with joy.]*

What is obvious is that Victoria, and her peer facilitators, invited participants to teach each other by asking them explicitly to reflect on their own background experiences; and, then facilitated dialogue on what they knew, how they knew it, and what they considered to be engaging ideas as a result. This is generally true of their work across all modules. For example, in a module on Literacy and Numeracy, another facilitator, Concepción asked, "What do you all do in your house to support the development of literacy in the children [in your care]?" One woman responded, "[q]ue me cuenten una historia," and, someone else offered, "que se emocionen a leer." (Observation, March 28, 2005) She shifted between the use of a curriculum guide activity and authentic conversation about real situations and understandings to sustain the dialogue on connections between real children in their care, real experiences with oral and written language and official mandates on literacy. Further, in a module on Health and Safety, Victoria prompted: "How can I prevent illness? Does anyone have a policy?" One woman explained, "When they're sick, I call their parents because they can't stay; it'll spread." Immediately all participants organize themselves into small group and begin sharing personal stories. Victoria notes how the sudden talk flows into various conversations. Then as these conversations wane to a pause, one woman discloses that she witnessed a doctor diagnose chicken pox as dandruff. As she listens, Victoria distributes Southwest State Kids pamphlets; and, she comments, as soon as the woman is finished and all pamphlets are handed out: "If you have kids without insurance, this is a service that provides low-cost medical services, such as eye-ware, dental, medical, ..." As a few women make anxious comments about how they notice young parents are often distracted from keeping a close watch on infants, Victoria further emphasizes, "Yes, never leave infants in carriers, on tables; a lot of young parents...." (Observation Notes, February 19, 2005) But one participant contributes before Victoria can finish her sentence, "But, daughters don't listen to their mothers!" And, then everyone bursts into a laughter that signals both relief and understanding.

Moreover, what is particularly salient from this work, is the manner by which the facilitators addressed participants different contributions (e.g., stories, conundrums, dichos, moral imperatives, questions, etc.) to shape teaching and learning.

There are connections between the participants and each other, participants and the facilitators, and vice versa. Participants are clearly listening to what the providers prompt, question, and suggest in order to decide what they will bring forward on behalf of the families and children in their care. Intersected with this, facilitators listen carefully to what the providers' disclosures, questions, and suggestions in order to address the needs they bring forward on behalf of the families and children in their care. Through such a deliberate and reflexive process, providers pointed to various needs and facilitators determined how to address these needs, as well as make needed connections to official expectations mandated for the program.

In sum, Charlas was originally conceptualized as a 16 clock-hour training course for in-home family child care providers to enrich the quality of early in-home care for thousands children in response to both the steadily increasing numbers of very young children who are cared for by kith and kin in homes all across the state, and a more sweeping national agenda for authorizing future funding. This project was indeed shaped by special interests to 1) set standards for in-home care provisions and, thereby, standardize early in-home care, 2) professionalize individuals who have had little, if any, formal training in early child care and education, and 3) establish a clear connection between this a priori school experience and the imminent universal pre-school advancement trend, in order to make sure all children come to school ready to learn. Its final revision as 18-hour course was developed as the state-wide implementation training course; the expectation was that it would include a standard curriculum for training in-home providers whether they resided in remotely rural areas (e.g., the Navajo Nation and the northern Pueblos) or growing urban centers (e.g., Alhambra and Las Golondrinas).

Its implementation, over the course of nine months, was studied from a narrative framework, because the underpinnings of *conversation* relate directly to both the notions of story and dialogue, which are critical features of narrative inquiry and thinking about things narratively. Three research questions focused on the design and implementation of the course by framing data collection and analysis on the enactment of the curriculum guide in tandem with the conversations among course participants. This narrative analysis highlighted four key findings—the need for conceptual, conversation and cultural competence in learning, for relevant learning, for learning in a community, and for addressing the needs of children and their families. Across the charlas courses there were different, but equally challenging, tensions around speaking to cultural and conceptual competence while at the same time facilitating fluid and focused conversations. Nonetheless, it was also obvious that the use of conversation as a medium for addressing the curriculum invoked a deeper personal and professional engagement by participants.

Making Their Way Across a Rugged Landscape

For all intents and purposes, narratives about the conceptual design for the facilitators' curriculum guide were remarkably similar in composition. These featured uniform references to essential components for the course: an introductory letter; lesson plans; a list of relevant material resources; a scope and sequence for introducing the module, starting conversations, and continuing conversations; a list of key questions to focus the module; prompts to initiate participation in an activity and others to expand participation; and a synthesizing activity for each module. There was also a clear emphasis on the economy of the handbook in terms of how it could be used to train both trainers (i.e., experienced and credentialed family child care professionals who would serve as course facilitators) and trainees (i.e., in-home family child care providers taking the 18-hour course) across vastly different contexts and situations with in-home child care providers.

But in terms of its enactment, narratives revealed palpable tensions around: (1) using written literacy for activities and evaluations and (2) framing implementation of the curriculum. Those involved in designing the handbook equivocated between relying on extended uses of conventional writing and expecting professionals to be comfortable using writing to express themselves. And, the uncertainty about how precisely to direct facilitators' use of the curriculum guide had to do with uncertainty about the skillfulness of facilitators to achieve course aims. In the end, the curriculum guide was filled with prescriptions for each of the eighteen hours and a standardized written evaluation form was produced. Nonetheless, an *unofficial* recognition emerged that the facilitators would come to know and understand the providers and their needs, and they would align this with the curriculum.

Narratives, then, were composed with multiple meanings and purposes and functions. Some were seemingly even and smooth, giving the impression of clarity about the goal of the state to improve early child care and education and the form the course should take to accomplish that goal. Others, however, presented a gritty texture, showing where experiences, meanings, perspectives and values did not align evenly, especially when intentional consideration was given to the cultural, linguistic, socio-economic, and political nature of the circumstances and lived experiences of providers, the children they care for and their families. Articulating these latter narratives involved unmistakable apprehension, much like the precaution sojourners take to secure their footing as when crossing furrowed terrain.

Thus the development and implementation of the Charlas course did not happen simply by following a logical plan, step by step, to reach the prescribed goals. Instead, the experience of each course usually emerged in the midst of providers' pressing challenges and concerns, their sense of confusion because of limited access to accurate information, and the plan for each curricular module. In such contested spaces, there were tensions experienced by all involved. These were not exacerbated emotions that escalated in defense of what was believed to be right; rather, these were moments of uncertainty around how make sense of different interests, perspectives and requirements. Through a back and forth process of listening and asking questions and figuring out how to confirm both emic and etic meanings, divergent realities came face to face at the boundaries that lay between. Perceptions were re-framed to include what may not have been anticipated, seemed to make sense, or was estimated as too much of a risk to consider. Facilitators seemed to wonder how to show their cariño, or genuine regard, in these delicate situations, yet at the same time respond appropriately and remain focused on the curriculum. These dialogical turns compelled participants to listen to each other, acknowledge one another's experience and perspective, and clarify the focus of the discussion. Moreover, participants contributed to conversations more clearly and deliberately when they realized these dialogical turns presented opportune moments for them to articulate relevant connections between their own personal and professional experiences and a particular curriculum topic.

It gradually became obvious, that when facilitators welcomed opportunities to speak directly and explicitly to what providers considered relevant (i.e., describing their unique situations, explaining their personal and cultural conceptualizations of providing excellent care for children, and reflecting on implications of state policy and program requirements), conversations reflected more continuous and critical engagement. This process involved a number of iterative exchanges; that is, posing questions, listening to responses, posing further questions, listening to additional responses, etc. Facilitators seemed to monitor how the rhythm of these changes waxed and waned in order to encourage further discussion and thinking about ideas and issues, or bring a conversation to closure. Further, facilitators searched for connections between what they heard—either in response to a specific prompt or even what was seemingly stated *out of the blue*—and overarching course goals. They paid particular attention to turns in the conversation and identified intersections between providers' references to immediate concerns and the curricular objectives of the module. In other words, facilitators learned how to locate providers' concerns and needs in a larger context, by listening; and, through listening, providers learned how to examine their own and others' concerns and needs in order to achieve new understanding on how to address these.

Lastly, sharing regard for one another as individuals, as well as the challenges they faced, whether similar or different, was of paramount importance to all. According to providers, this was the most assured way to meet their needs. They explained over and over that the process of coming together, forging relationships among all participants, and learning how to talk about crucial concerns and questions required engagement in process as well as a change in perspective on how to view oneself, one's peers, and the work both do. As such a process was forged, participants knew that they were regarded with respect and sensitivity and belonged in the group. Moreover, their reflections on creating a sense of community honored the work they all had been doing, made it possible to challenge each other to listen and share, and a broader base of encouragement to continue learning. In their terms, this demonstrated genuine care for one another and constituted a necessary condition for being a community and being able to learn. Conversations were indeed communal, conceptual and dialogic; the participants' diverse voices and experiences, the facilitators' perceptions and interpretations, and the course curriculum resonated across, in between and throughout these vocal spaces.

There was, however, one lingering question that remained unanswered. This had to do with the desire to keep connected beyond the 18 hours of training, or any other professional development event for that matter. All participants were particularly concerned about returning to the regularities of their work because they primarily felt isolated in these situations. For them, figuring out how to carry forward the sense of community they created and shared, and how to nurture that over time became a compelling priority.

References

The 2007 child care licensing study. (2009). *National Association for Regulatory Administration and National Child Care Information and Technical Assistance Center.* http://www.naralicensing.org/displaycommon.cfm?an=1&subarticlenbr=160. (retrieved August 24, 2010)

Alverman, D. (2000). Narrative Research. In M. Kamil, P. Mosenthal, R. Barr and P.D.Pearson (Eds.), *Handbook reading research.* Mahwah, NJ: Lawrence Earlbaum Publishers, Inc.

Bakhtin, M. (1981). *The dialogic imagination.* Austin: University of Texas, Press.

Barone, T. (2007). A return to the gold standard? Questioning the future of narrative con struction as educational research. *Qualitative Inquiry*, 13, 454-470.

Care for school-age children. (1999). *Annie E. Casey Foundation.* http://www.aecf.org/org/pulications/child/fam.htm. (retrieved April 4, 2006)

Chase, S.E. (2005). Narrative inquiry: Multiple lenses, approaches, voices. In Denzin, N.K., &Lincoln, Y.S. (Eds.), *The sage handbook of qualitative research.* (3rd Ed). (pp. 651-679). Thousand Oaks, CA: Sage.

Clandenin, J. & M. Connelly. (2000). *Narrative inquiry. Experience and story in qualitative research.* San Francisco: Jossey-Bass, Inc. Publishers.

Gonzalez-Mena, J. (2012). Child, family and community: *Family centered early care and education.* San Francisco: Pearson, Inc.

Ladson Billings, G. (2001). Racialized Discourses and Ethnic Epistemologies. In N. Denzin & Y.Lincoln (Eds.), pp.398-432. *The landscape of qualitative research.* Thousand Oaks, CA: Sage Publications, Inc.

Love, J. M., et al., (2003), Child Care Quality Matters: How Conclusions May Vary With Context. *Child Development*, 74: 1021–1033.

Professional development for care givers. (1999). *Annie E. Casey Foundation.* http://www.aecf.org/org/pulications/child/fam.htm. (retrieved April 4, 2006)

Shanton, K. & T. Valenzuela. (2005). Not in the Script: What Parent, Student and Teacher Have to Say About the Success of Success For All. In L. Poyner & P. Wolfe (Eds.), *Marketing fear in America's public schools.* Mahwah, NJ: Lawrence Earlbaum Publishers, Inc.

Shonkoff, J. & D. Phillips. (2000). *From neurons to neighborhoods. The science of early childhood devel opment.* Washington, DC: National Academy Press.

State of America's children 2005 report. (2005). *Children's Defense Fund.* http://www.childrensdefense.org/ss. (retrieved April 4, 2006)

The NICHD study of early child care. (1998). *National Institutes of Child Health and Human Development.* Bethesda, MD.

Notes

[1] The hourly rate is often one half that of the national minimum wage.

[2] More than one in four families with young children earns an annual salary less than $25,000, and a family with both parents working full-time at the minimum wage earns only $21,400 a year).

[3] *Registered family child care* is defined by the New Mexico Administrative Code as "the residence of an independent caregiver who registers the home under these regulations to participate in the child and adult care food program or as a vendor in the state and

federal child care assistance programs." NMAC, 8.17.2.7.I. Registered providers are not licensed.

[4] It was hypothesized in a list of assumptions for this proposal that the "collaborative link" to Head Start "may [have] be[en] one of the best ways to increase provider training, increase Head Start capacity and improve quality of care in family child care homes."

[5] Members of the HPI workgroup represented the Office of Child Development (OCD),
Family Nutrition Bureau (FNB), Child Care Services Bureau (CCSB) and Head Start.

[6] A summary of "FCC Kith & Kin Issues" was prepared and distributed to workgroup members via facsimile.

[7] The agreements and assumptions for the *HPI* workgroup are recorded in an official Memorandum for Decision Deputy Director, CYFD, to Deputy Secretary, CYFD, December 17, 2001.

[8] This was based on a actual experience with a FNB professional seminar in which the trainer made such a recommendation for training non-professionals.

[9] According to Baptiste and Reyes, there have been discussions with CYFD staff about the possibility of creating a series of courses, leveled much like a career ladder model, and preparing NM kids for the state's movement toward universal preschool and K-12 school readiness, all of which would begin with the 18-hour course Charlas. At the time of their interviews, however, funding was not available for developing such supplementary levels.

[10] The documentation of "notes from the parking lot" was not dated exactly, nor provided any reference the author; however, citations of future dates, for achieving goals, suggest that it was composed just before the two Family Child Care Specialists assumed the lead in implementing and the remainder of the pilot training sessions.

[11] The transcription is drawn from a facilitator journaling, and was edited only to reflect the more natural flow of conversation between the two facilitators and the research assistant. (Facilitator Journaling, January 21, 2005).

[12] The question of how the 18-hour course benefited families and children is addressed here. Given that the focus of the evaluation was on the course, not on the actual homes of the providers, the data drawn for this analysis comes from the explicit interactions among and between the providers and participants in class.

CHAPTER THREE
"'YOU'RE DOING THE BEST WITH WHAT YOU HAVE.'
'NO, WE DO WITH WHAT WE DON'T HAVE.'"

Victoria Cadena, La Visión Institute

For more than three years, I spent time working with many colleagues at the La Visión Institute and Southwest State University to create and implement the 18-Hour Family Child Care Provider Course, *Charlas*. I became involved in this work because I was an experienced child care provider, had lived in the area all of my life and believed I could communicate with providers so that we could make a difference together. I was excited because it was a new project and it was being done for the first time. At the same time, I was worried that I wasn't going to be able to meet the needs of the participants. But, over time, I grew more empathetic because as I learned more about them I gained respect for the creative and complex ways they managed their circumstances and educated the children in their care.

In this chapter, I share how I came to understand my work with family child care providers. This process was complicated by the struggle to address mandates related to state law and respecting my longing to be true to what family child care providers and their communities want for children, especially related to their language and culture.

Following Mandates and Responding to Needs

The goal of the course was to provide a new option to meet the recent state legislation on professional development—of six clock hours per year—for family child care providers. They needed to document participation in professional development in order to continue receiving access to social services and food subsidy to support the children they cared for. In addition to meeting the clock hour requirements, the Office of Child Development (OCD) wanted providers to acquire a basic—but also different—understanding of quality child care.

My intention was to both facilitate the course according to its prescribed curriculum and honor the particular backgrounds and needs of different family child care providers. It was important to me that they understand the essential elements in quality child care, because of the particular support needed during the first three years of a child's life. But, I also realized providers already demonstrated many of these elements in their care. They cared deeply about children. The challenges they faced were not the result of a complete lack of understanding.

However, I don't think, they realized the profound effect their care had on children's long-term development and well-being. Also, knowing that a majority of children in Southwest State were being cared for by family, and that family care providers were caring for their relatives' children, it was important for me to ground my work with them in the these particular contexts, as well as more broadly in their language and culture.

Negotiating Between Complying and Advocating

Charlas was designed as a professional development opportunity for family child care providers, mandated as an 18-hour course by Southwest State in 2003. My main role was to guide the implementation of the course—from the pilot test to evaluation. The majority of my work in this process involved managing a long line of particular, although sometimes overlapping, activities:

- recruiting family child care providers;
- organizing course schedules and appropriate materials;
- communicating regularly and repeatedly with interested providers;
- facilitating *charlas* with family child care providers as we explored the required curriculum;
- reviewing participants' reflections on individual modules and the course as a whole; and, assessing provider-child interactions in the home.

I found recruiting to be the most challenging of these because I remember thinking, "Okay, I need in-home care providers. How do I go about finding them?" I decided to collaborate with the Community Action Agency (CAA) and Child Youth and Families Department (CYFD). These agencies listed family child care providers who were identified as unsatisfactory in terms of their licensure or registration status. Recruiting was focused on these providers because there was an accessible directory and they needed this kind of support to continue. I also talked to representatives in both agencies and acquired contact information for new providers who had successfully gone through their orientations. Because all providers had to meet the criterion of annual professional development, *Charlas* was relevant to both licensed and registered providers. So, my recruiting strategy was crafted as a particular response to both state regulation and provider need.

I combed through the list of providers, and I began by calling the ones I knew. Even though we were just talking on the phone, I always wanted to reconnect first:

Bueno, soy Victoria. Hace mucho tiempo que no hablamos. ¿Qué tal?
...
¿Cómo están los niños?
...
You know, we have this course and it's 18 hours. One of the incentives is that you could use some of the hours in order to meet this year's professional development requirement and then roll over hours towards next year's requirement.
...

After I made these contacts, I felt much more comfortable. I then called providers I didn't know. These next conversations were very different because I had to approach the individuals by focusing first on the benefits of the course rather than drawing on the trust of an already established relationship.

For those on the waiting list who couldn't be included right away, I wanted to make sure that they didn't lose interest. So, I frequently called to reassure them that they were at the top of the waiting list and offered information on the next course. Without exception, they assured me how much my call meant to them.

In the very beginning, I had mixed feelings about recruiting. I felt like I was advocating and soliciting. It was confusing: I had to become a sales person for *what a great course this was* as well as a counselor on *how it would meet their needs*. So, on the one hand I offered them materials they could use in their homes as incentives; and, on the other hand, I acknowledged the support they needed to fulfill requirements in order to continue working with children in their homes.

But, what stands out most clearly to me is how recruiting changed unexpectedly—almost the instant the first group of providers got involved. People were finding out about the course by word of mouth before I even announced the second course. It was like a domino effect. One provider would say to someone else she knew who was also providing family child care, "Oh, I took this really great course," and then that individual would contact me. It took on a life of its own. They were getting my number through this remarkable network. So, I ended up having a waiting list every time we were ready to start a new course.

Once recruiting a class was complete, I had to finalize the timeline and other logistics. I always anticipated scheduling the modules either during the weekend—on Saturdays—or in the evenings. This way the course would match when the providers were available because they weren't caring for children. Eventually, we added an assessment. It was based on all the same criteria that we used for *Charlas*; the only extra thing was that the participants knew we were going to go in and do an assessment (i.e., Child Care Assessment Tool for Relatives). They also received a stipend for accommodating this additional activity in the course and allowing us entry into their homes.

In the midst of scheduling, I also had to plan and prepare. I think I was very fortunate because I was able to order materials that I realized would be beneficial to the providers. For example, we would give them multiple books—that were bilingual and multicultural—when we did the language or literacy modules. During the health and safety modules they would get things like safety plug covers for outlets, thermometers for their refrigerators, knob covers for stove handles, latches to secure cabinet doors, and first aid kits. These were essential for quality care giving because providers needed these tools to lower the risks of children encountering accidental or unnecessary harm.

Prior to the course starting, I would call them twice—one month and one week—in advance. I would say, "This is just a reminder that the class starts soon. It's going to be....; and, we meet from...." I did this because it seemed like they needed encouragement. The providers were always so occupied by the needs and schedules of the children and families they served that sometimes they had a tendency to forget what they had put on the back burner. I thought maybe they would feel frustrated that they knew ahead of time what was going to happen and, therefore, less interested to show up and participate. But looking back now, I think those reminders helped build a relationship. The phone calls provided a systematic and personal way to keep in touch. And, this continuous line of communication fostered conversations about their particular circumstances, interests, and questions. For example, they would talk about whether there were emotional hardships because children were starting school—anything that might present difficulties with attending class. They were very open to talking about their personal lives, their family, or unexpected problems. It was amazing. So I knew that even though I didn't have a picture of what that person looked like, I had a name, a sense of the home situation, and a connection to continuing the conversation. Despite the fact that I could not put a face with a name until that first module, I actually had useful prior knowledge of their backgrounds and whether they were caring for children with special needs, their grandchildren, or whatever the case may have been.

Moreover, I felt I could relate to them because some of the same experiences that they were talking about I had gone through myself. We shared so many touchstones. In most of the families there were adult children; I had adult children. We were of similar ages and generations; I was a grandmother caring for my grandson. I, too, was struggling to go to school; I was Hispanic. So, I could honestly relate to their experiences. I think all of that mattered in developing our relationships and accomplishing the work in the course. I understood how they felt so I could connect with and support them.

By the start of the course, I knew many of them and their situations. We had already been introduced.

Each of the modules had a question I would ask or a prompt that was supposed to promote dialogue. The goal was to create a forum for sharing relevant experiences by each of the providers. One of the dialogues that was most memorable was health and safety in the second, or third, course. Although child abuse was one of the topics recommended for discussion, I would never have predicted what happened in our dialogue. The providers were so willing to share and some of them revealed they had been abused in different ways—verbally, physically, and sexually. They listened to each other compassionately. This so surprised me that it profoundly shaped my view of the value of unexpected possible conversations. I realized that was one of my strengths: to be able to support the providers to create an open space where they could just share and/or listen. When things came up that were complicated or painful, I encouraged them to focus the conversation on the topic and be empathetic.

I don't think it was so much what I said, but it was how I said it. I was very respectful of the process that emerged in our dialogues. I didn't cut them off. I waited for them to share. They were able to talk and ask questions without being interrupted. I also shared my personal reflections on similar kinds of experiences. When they paused and seemed to look to me to participate, too. So they had a sense of "Oh, she's human, she's had these same experiences." Together we reminded each other of our connectedness in this work and world.

I could see that they valued this by the way they treated each other's vulnerability. Sometimes the ones that didn't share in the beginning of a module dialogue were the ones that either shared at the end of the module or wrote explicit reflections in their course evaluation. No one pointed out who did or did not talk. It was as if they were finding the least obstructed pathways to follow in order to get to a clearing and talk more openly. I read their feedback to myself after every module and found private ways to acknowledge such contributions.

It was amazing because the conversation always seemed to be there. I can't remember a single time when there wasn't any talk or the participation seemed totally empty. If there had been several awkward silences, I would make a conscious effort to facilitate a little bit differently the next time we talked. Maybe I would pair them up to get started, hoping to encourage the ones who wouldn't automatically talk in front of the whole group to be more comfortable to share, as well as have plenty of ideas to then talk about together as a whole group.

I was putting a lot of time and energy into developing conversations this way. But, I think the benefits outweigh the time and energy that were put in. It wasn't just the materials that they were receiving but it was the interaction among the providers and the understanding they created or renewed through the relationships they developed together. I always heard them comment, maybe not at the first class but by the third or fourth module that they actually looked forward to attending the classes and learning.

So, the feedback I got was also rewarding. It wasn't instantaneous, but in the end it stressed how much they really had enjoyed the experience in Charlas. The common response after the providers completed the course was they didn't anticipate that they would get so much out of it. I thought,

> *Oh my gosh, this is a success! This is really having an impact on providers. I'm not having to solicit them because they're finding that they are willing to take the course and get so much out of it.*

I never felt like I was criticized, and I didn't take their feedback personally. I always reminded myself that the person giving me any feedback is coming from her own place and her own time. I respected their opinions and reflections.

In addition to participating in the course modules, providers were assessed on all the core competencies of the curriculum. There were two assessments scheduled before we began the course: one prior to the first course module and one after we finished. In an orientation meeting, that usually lasted about two hours, we discussed how I would go into their homes and do the assessments. When I would go into their homes, I would sample ten different areas of interaction between the provider and children using the Child Care Assessment Tool for Relatives.

During the assessment, I sat and observed a number of interactions between the provider and the children in timed intervals with focuses on categories of care. I would check off certain indicators on my form after each interval and in between the different samplings. The only thing I was looking for was behavior related to the prescribed criteria. There was no interaction between the provider and me or the children and me. Because they knew who I was, it wasn't really a surprise to them. I think that they were very comfortable most of the time.

Eventually, I decided to re-shape the first module to include a basic orientation so that they would have a chance to talk with peers right from the start about the general curriculum outline, expectations of the Child Youth Family Department and any house rules we wanted or needed. Rather than just streamlining the process of getting started, this actually embedded the technicality of an assessment orientation into the lifeline of our conversations. We discussed what they should expect during the whole process. It was a way to practice the integrity of our aims for dialogue with every aspect of the course.

Sorting Through Memories and Feelings

When I think back on the experiences, I have a flood of memories. There were so many individuals, and their contributions to the course were as diverse as the situations in which they lived and provided care for children. They were of different abilities, ages, attitudes, cultural backgrounds, ethnicities, faiths, genders, interests, languages, learning styles, and needs.

There was one provider, Guiselle Barranza, I often think about. She was an older woman; she must have been in her late sixties. Guiselle was providing care for her grandchildren and a couple of other younger neighborhood children. I remember doing the home visits to complete the CCATR. She lived in a mobile home. I had some background on her situation because we had done an interview prior to the visit. I knew that originally Guiselle had only cared for her son's children. At the time of the home visit, however, he had been incarcerated. So, she ended up with custody of the children. Guiselle was unexpectedly put in that predicament. In order to support her family, she had to become the children's guardian. One of her granddaughters, who was in high school, was living with her. I remember the conversation we had about the challenges trying to support her granddaughter by wanting her to take college classes, caring for her grandchildren, and being concerned for her son.

I think one of the things I can't forget was that she was fluent in Spanish and English, but didn't read or write English. So, here I was, doing one of the CCATR tasks that focuses on literacy and the evidence of books in the home. Despite her complicated circumstances and small house, I remember Guiselle was telling her grandchildren how rich they were. She made a point of having books for the children. Even though I knew she couldn't read the words, she pointed them out. She would also have the children look carefully at the pictures and she would point too. And they would name them together.

We always have an idea of what is appropriate and what providers should have —and it is a rich language and literacy environment. I just remember how startling the situation was for me. After looking at a few books, she engaged in conversation with one of the children. There was a birdcage in her mobile home and she was talking to the child about the bird. Guiselle pulled out a figure that the children had made. It was only made out of natural objects from the environment like, twigs, tree needles, and bark. It was exquisite. There were so many words and images shared between Guiselle and the child in that conversation. As I listened to this conversation and watched Guiselle interact with the child, I couldn't help think that what she had done was connect our conversation in the literacy module about creativity and art with what she had in her home. Moreover, I had an epiphany, thinking to myself, "Would I, as a parent, have my own grandchildren cared for by this individual?" Again, although she didn't read or write, these interactions with the children about naming pictures, looking at words, and building the model of the bird were invaluable.

That was a very profound experience for me. I gained clarity on my own perspective and found that I had to amplify my view. I realized I couldn't fit literacy into the neat little box or compartmentalize it. Instead I had to see it as dynamic and as something that happens between people when they interact with words and images through different kinds of language.

Guiselle passed away almost a year after. I remember how poignant that was. I think I read her obituary in the newspaper. So, I went to the memorial service. Her granddaughter remembered me, and I knew who many of the visitors were. I was trying to put stories together that Guiselle had told about her family life. It was funny because I felt like I knew the friends and family members who were there but they had no clue who I was or how much I knew about them. This makes me wonder at how we can often be mistaken about what someone knows.

I think this experience hits so close to home because Guiselle shared more openly and captured our attention. Situations like this helped all of us understand more clearly why we became providers and the differences in our lives that shaped our experiences as providers.

I also remember another woman, Cecilia Chavez, who talked about how she learned to read. She explained that it had to do with growing up in Chiapas, Mexico, and traveling around the city by bus almost every day. She had to ride the camiones, or buses, in order to get back and forth across town. And, she remembered learning to read by reading the signs on and in the buses. She described looking at the pictures pasted on the outside of the buses and above the seats inside. She explained how she needed to make sense of the letters and words in order to know where to go and how to get there. She recounted how she often talked to people on the buses about what the signs said. So, she learned to read not in a school setting, but by traveling around the city, doing what was essential to her daily survival.

We also talked from time to time about other ways of learning. In particular, we debated the importance of culture and family traditions. We acknowledged how these provided different ways to learn to read and write. For me, nevertheless, I can't forget how we made that connection for ourselves but not always for the children in our care. And, we learned from each other.

For me, the most important sign of success was the reciprocated respect between facilitators and participants. We explicitly validated the importance of our different experiences and the commitment to families and children we share.

Being True to Ourselves and Our Families

The opportunity to reflect on my experiences has given me insight into the misalignment between traditional methods of informing people about policy and practice in a workshop and the dialogues among child care providers. First and foremost, I had to alter the curriculum plan to make it fit our work rather than make our work fit the curriculum plan. I couldn't follow the methodology exactly as suggested in the facilitator's guide. The method that emerged from my work with these remarkable individuals was shaped by our conversations about the curriculum guide, which were shaped by experiences we had with children and the relationships we developed with each other, as well as the guide.

Basically, a traditional methodology is based on the expectation that individuals talk about their experiences and ideas in prescribed terms—using vocabulary and meanings that may not be familiar or useful to them. In other words, a traditional methodology does not call for someone to talk first about her experiences and ideas in her own language or require a facilitator to think about the relevance of what she offers to the curriculum. The insight I gleaned from reflection is that by starting with the curriculum, rather than an individual, is much more difficult to make sense of what to talk about and how to talk to each other.

My reflection has further shown me that when we talked using terms that were familiar to us—words that belonged to our language and we had confidence in using—we not only could understand each other, but we were able to take on new words and ideas because we made them work for us.

Nevertheless, I tried to follow the format and stay true to the facilitator's guide as much as possible. But, there were times when I had to improvise.

I remember facilitating module eight, and a number of times participants found the word *acquisition* to be strange. I thought to myself, "Who created this, or thought this would be appropriate for these providers?" It sounded so simple, but when I used that word, participants kept asking me what it meant even though I had defined it more than once. So, I eventually began to leave it out in our first conversation about language acquisition. But, I used it once we had talked about how surprising it always was how quickly children learned new words and phrases. As we talked about our own ideas, we also talked about the theories of child language acquisition. I rephrased our familiar words as acquisition in order to connect the curriculum to providers' language and thinking instead of the other way around.

Again, even though acquisition was the correct term, we needed to take into consideration how the providers thought about language and the words they used first. By the end of the module I was using the word acquisition when we talked about children's language, and they weren't asking me about the term. They had even started to experiment with their own use of the word to describe what they noticed about children's language.

I reflected on this by thinking, "Okay, here I am telling providers to read to children and so forth, but my mother never read to me. So, I obviously came to not only learn to read but want to read, without my mother doing what the facilitator's guide told me to suggest." I think the misalignment here is between what should be and what is. Once I realized that, I came up with my own personal examples to convey how reading was acquired without calling it first acquisition. I reflected on how I learned to read and I shared those experiences with them; I remembered learning how to read by reading signs; I learned by having to know which bus to take. I didn't have the recommended childhood where your mother sat you down and read you stories before bedtime.

The providers' had assumed that children learned language by being taught certain words and phrases, not so much conversation, or by using language together. When we talked about the different ways that they were actually providing multiple experiences for children, especially playing and talking with them about whatever was on their mind. So, in our conversations they realized what their assumptions were limited, and they made new connections. It was in the context of our dialogues about family, culture, and daily routines.

Instead of my work being about implementing best practices, my work was about dynamic practices—cultural, familial, and personal—that best illustrated how we care about children, do different things with them and learn with them in order to support them.

CHAPTER FOUR
LISTENING: A CHANNEL FOR CRITICAL LITERACY

Kyle D. Shanton, Albion College
Victoria Cadena, La Visión Institute

And, what can be learned from the different stories told by participants and facilitators involved in *Charlas*? When Victoria and I look back at these stories, we realize there are, of course, many more things to be learned than we can count or name. Nonetheless, the most salient lessons are that: conversations were sometimes in English, sometimes in Spanish and other times in both; conversations called for participants to listen intentionally to each other as they elaborated concerns, expectations and needs; listening called for honoring both the personal and the professional because these were inseparably connected and understanding one required understanding the other; listening facilitated repeated clarification and revision of understandings of different circumstances, interests and needs; listening engendered new perspectives on recognizing, and respecting similarities and differences in circumstances, interests and needs; and, listening consistently reflected a sense of welcome and belonging as well as a desire to continue having a conversations as a professional community beyond the *Charlas* experience. Listening stirred everyone to give on-going sensitive and serious consideration to policy initiatives, implications for practice, and the significance of self-determination in relation to both. Realizing these lessons was possible because participants and facilitators intentionally focused their attention, reflection and action on doing so. And, as they all pointed out, listening channeled that process.

Access to Many Stories

As Chimamanda Adichie elaborated (TED Talk, July 10, 2009), it is essential that we have access to many stories, because without plurality we place ourselves in danger of accepting the limits of what one version suggests is *real* or *just the way it is*. A single story limits what we might be able to do for ourselves, as well as with and for each other. A single story does not provide the intellectual space or materials needed to sort through discrepancies and differences among individual experiences, interests or needs. However, having access to numerous stories brings into view the fact that the landscapes of our own and others' lived experiences are expansive and full of variety about *what is real* and *how to understand it*. Having multiple stories helps us come to more logical and practical terms about what is at stake, what matters, whether or not the subject of the story pertains to our particular circumstances, and how to figure out what the options might be for addressing it if it is pertinent. Having access to numerous stories helps realize that both similarities and differences are *real* or *the way it is*, and neither the precludes the other: diversity provides the conditions needed to develop pluralism in perspective and critical consciousness in thinking.

In *Charlas*, listening was a medium to invoke attention, reflection and action because it was channeled connections across lived experiences, knowledge and understanding. Participants' diverse needs and vulnerabilities for providing family child care were not excluded or marginalized by the presentation of a single, official view of family child care; their impressions of how to proceed in the face of daily challenges and policy changes were not framed by an overwhelming sense that what someone else knew was either better or what actually mattered. Instead, Victoria, her colleagues and participants directed their individual and collective attention and reflection to conjoin many narratives into the curriculum of their work together. In this way they began to realize there was a repertory of relevant experiences and views of family child care. The official narrative—whether it be a policy mandate or a curriculum guide—was definitely present: it was a priority for participants across discussion, reflection and action. Notwithstanding, it was but one of many narratives. And, participants' individual and collective listening helped reframe their understandings and views to help stir new action.

With only a single story about family child care, there would not have been extensive discussion and reflection on the challenges of communicating explicitly with family members about fair business practice and its implications for ultimately meeting children's needs and providing ongoing child care; there would not have been sensitive and sophisticated dialogue about various issues of child abuse and neglect in terms of how to notice these as well as communicate accordingly; there would not have been clear and varied illustrations of acknowledging and responding accurately and directly to children's language and literacy. Listening to many stories made this possible.

A Medium for Attention, Reflection and Action

Katherine Schultz (2003) used the term listening to mean more than just hearing. For her, listening pertains to how a teacher attends to children, youth, and their families. She explained, "I purposefully choose to focus on listening to highlight the centrality of relationships in teaching. Observation can be done from a distance, listening requires proximity and intimacy."(p.8) Schultz also suggested that listening fosters the development of relationships and brings all involved closer to one another as they reflect on each other's contributions to the conversations they shared. Further, listening necessitates action because, in order to listen, you must participate intentionally in a communicative act. Victoria and I saw the very same thing as we examined the various narratives about *Charlas*.

For example, in the midst of the work, it seemed to always surprise us that there were multiple points of entry into, as well as modes of participation in, the conversations. We mistakenly anticipated that several who did not talk right away would probably remain quiet throughout the course. However, our assumptions were challenged over and over again. At the start of every class session, there were a number of seemingly silent participants. But, by the end of each session those on the periphery of the conversation had stepped forward to cross that imagined boundary, articulating reflections on their peers' contributions and posing their own questions, as well as planting new ideas to consider. There were also those who spoke less during the whole group conversations, but more either in small groups or with several different individuals right after the class session. As Nichols (1995) explained, "You don't change relationships by trying to control other people's behavior, but by changing yourself in relation to them." (p.243) The deliberate and direct focus on listening embodied such an understanding among many, if not all, involved. Thus, Victoria and I have come to realize that those seemingly silent participants had indeed been listening: How else could they have been able to engage their perhaps more outspoken peers so explicitly and meaningfully, in such different ways, while also reflecting the relevance of the conversation to their own needs and situations?

Schultz also acknowledged that listening involves signaling; that is, by making a confirming statement or asking a question or nodding, you demonstrate to the person who is talking that you are present, that you hear her or him, and that you are trying to connect, or would like to contribute, fervidly and genuinely. However, she cautioned that listening is also evident in what happens beyond any immediate or observable signaling. Similarly, Brady (2003) explained that, "…the quiet mind makes possible an overall awareness of the total situation, including ourselves." (p. 120)

Similarly, we see how listening shaped not only the conversations during the *Charlas* course, but also the work of individuals following the course (Gonzalez-Mena, 2012). Victoria's story of the observation with Guiselle—in which she saw her talking with her grandchildren about books they had read together, the bird cage in her trailer home, and making the craft as they talked together—is one such example. While the point here is not to say that implementing the course curriculum caused her to add these things to her practice, it is clearly evident that her interaction and conversation with her grandchild reflected her intentional focus on different questions about and illustrations of literacy in conversations with her peers and Victoria in her *Charlas* experience. Nichols (1995) described it this way: "Friends who listen make us feel interesting, and their interest inspires us to say more interesting things." (p.226) By attending to the words and meanings of her peer interlocutors, and knowing that her peers attended to her words and meanings, Guiselle became determined to figure out which literacy ideas were most accessible and relevant, as well as how to enact these in her practice.

As Victoria noted previously, there were several occasions on which conversations focused on cultivating a shared sense of relationships; these required talking to one another over and over again, exchanging examples from different lived experiences, identifying similarities across experiential boundaries, as well as demonstrating genuine regard for what was indeed different. Listening channeled their confirmations of such commitments. Notwithstanding, it is both interesting and important to note that participants were neither required nor urged to speak or agree during any conversation. Again, there were multiple ways to enter into and participate in the conversations.

For us, then, listening necessitated action on the part of everyone involved. That action took different forms and followed different paces. Nonetheless, all these various actions emerged out of paying critically conscious attention: providers and facilitators attended to each other's words, learned more about each other, adjusted their stance toward one another, realized questions they needed to ask about the issues at hand, as well as explored how they might take next steps in their own practice.

Synthesis and Self-determination

Listening served as a touchstone for the conversations among Victoria, her colleagues at La Visión and family child care practitioners participating in the *Charlas* courses. In order to listen, they had to engage each other in close and continuous communication—attending to each other's stories and questions about policy and reflecting on what these might mean for family child care and their practice. Such intensive engagement required them to re-position themselves in relation to self and those around them. By listening, *Charlas* participants were able to acknowledge and reconcile similarities and differences across their feelings, hunches, ideas, perspectives and questions and generate new possibilities for understanding and practice. By listening, *Charlas* participants were able them to name and assay the nature and presence of power in their work as family child care practitioners. Listening then also led them to synthesis—through listening they re-directed and re-framed their individual and collective gazes on the relationships between themselves and policy, themselves and their practices, as well as among each other as family child care practitioners.

Similar to the self-determination by Navajo teachers in the Rough Rock Demonstration Project (McCarty, 2003), family child care practitioners involved in *Charlas* engaged in critical reflection on their current context and exercised self-governance in order to name and enact their commitments to practice. They carefully considered how they understood, and determined how else they might understand, family child care policy and their practice in relation to it. Further, they valued sharing their various practices and next steps, as well as their intention to remain connected in conversations beyond the course.

As they listened, they made deliberate decisions to regard one's own and each other's words spoken aloud, to articulate shared and unshared meanings, and to put insights into practice in the midst of risk and uncertainty. They proportioned space and time needed to synthesize their various reflections and realize a process of determining together the next steps they would take as individual, and as a collective of, family child care practitioners.

References

Adichie, C. (TED Talk; July 10, 2009).
 http://www.ted.com/talks/chimamanda_adichie_the_danger_of_a_single_story. (retrieved May 31, 2014)
Annie E Casey Foundation. (2007). Retrieved on September 17, 2007 from
 http://www.aecf.org. (retrieved December 11, 2010).
Anzaldúa, G. (1999). *Borderlands/La Frontera: The new mestiza* (3rd edition). San Francisco: Aunt Lute Books.
Au, K. (1993). *Literacy instruction in multicultural settings.* Belmont, CA: Wadsworth/Thompson Learning.
Brady, M. (2003). *The wisdom of listening.* Somerville, MA: Wisdom Publications.
Gonzalez-Mena, J. (2012). Child, family and community: *Family centered early care and education.* San Francisco: Pearson, Inc.
Schulz, K. (2003). *Listening: A framework for teaching across differences.* New York: Teachers College Press.
McCarty, T. (2004). *A place to be Navajo: Rough Rock and the struggle for self-determination in indigenous schooling.* Mahwah, NJ: Lawrence Erlbaum Associates, Inc.
Nichols, M. (1995). *The lost art of listening: How learning to listen can improve relationships.* New York: The Guilford Press.

SERIES TWO

LITERACY DEMANDS ON NEW MEXICO TEACHERS AND STUDENTS: CONTEXT, PERSPECTIVE, AND HOPE

CHAPTER FIVE
DEMANDS OF OFFICIAL PORTRAITS

Richard J. Meyer, University of New Mexico

> There is little talk of the power of teaching, of this remarkable kind of human relationship, honored in all cultures. In our time, teaching is acknowledged as important but is often defined as a knowledge-delivery system. Yet teaching carries with it the obligation to understand the people in one's charge, to teach subject matter and skills, but also to inquire, to nurture, to have a sense of who a student is. (Rose, 2009, p. 168)

The use of portraiture (Lawrence-Lightfoot & Davis, 1997) as a research tool is not new, but its use as advocacy is increasingly important given the current education policy context. Portraiture has become a strategy by which education researchers illustrate the struggles that culturally and socially marginalized groups engage to declare the significance of their presence and voice. Lawrence-Lightfoot and Davis (1997) describe portraiture this way:

> As the researcher documents the context—rich with detailed description, anticipatory themes and metaphors, and allusions to history and evolution—she [sic] must remember that the context is not static and that the actors are not only shaped by the context, but that they also give it shape. The portraitist, then, must be vigilant in recording changes in the context, some as visible and anticipatable as the shifting seasons....Other changes in context are far more subtle...(p. 57).

In this series of essays, teachers, students, and I suggest that there is a grossly distorted portrait of students and teachers in New Mexico public schools and a need for a more accurate counterportrait. We do this by presenting the official portrait of schooling in the state—and of Mesa Vista Elementary School in particular—and re-presenting the situation through counterportraits based on participatory research that involved two teachers, two classrooms of students, and me over one school year (2006–2007).

In the official portrait, students' and teachers' identities, and the human relationships inherent in their teaching and learning together, are mathematically teased out— replaced by statistical indices (e.g., means and standard deviations) — in order to present a broad and sweeping picture. Such an image leaves the "obligation to understand the people in one's charge" (Rose 2009, p.168) far behind because of the demand to produce a broad and sweeping evaluation of performance and productivity. I refer to this first category as the *official portrait*, intentionally using a singular noun because there is only one such portrait. An official portrait has no room for specificity, the uniqueness of individual narratives, or an understanding of the multiple contexts in which children and teachers learn and teach. Its purpose is to draw lines around: which group or school is proficient and which is not, which gets more funding and which does not, and which makes Adequate Yearly Progress and which does not. Further, Goodman (2006) has argued that the current official portrait is textured with threats (e.g., reconstituting schools, prescribing curriculum, and multiplying intervals for evaluating student achievement) that are often realized, because of the political context of the 2001 reauthorization—No Child Left Behind—of the Elementary and Secondary Education Act (1965). The official portrait, in an increasing number of cases, has become essentially a yearly mug shot framed by particular partisan politics with definitions of what counts as legitimate.

I refer to the second category as *non-official portraits*, because these are not recognized in most official domains, such as district and state boards of education, legislative bodies, and foundations or granting agencies, and provide a counter point of view. Non–official portraits are plural in that these include multiple points of view, various kinds of data, different moments in time, and detailed cultural and linguistic illustrations. Rather than using static numerical indices to rank order students and schools according to performance differences, these counter-portraits are dynamic textual representations of children's and teachers' intellectual work together in the face of challenges. Non-official portraits are fluid pictures of lived experiences, composed and framed over time, rather than a still snapshot taken at one point in time. Composed of cultural, economic, ethnic, familial, community, linguistic, and religious narratives these portraits substantiate students' personal and school subjectivities (Moje, 2007). All of these are regarded as significant influences on student learning, performance and resilience. The non-official portraits presented here, then, are intentionally designed to counter the current official portrait. Non-official portraits feature thick descriptions (Geertz, 1973) by which the children and teachers participate with me in re-presenting themselves, their lives, including the people they love, and the words they have for all of this.

In the midst of the changing context they inhabit, New Mexico students, teachers, families, and legislators are all creating portraits about what matters. From my point of view, the emergence of multiple non-official portraits is a legitimate response to the erroneous presentation by the official portrait. I would not usually make a case for one category against another; however, my concern is that the official portrait is fundamentally mean-spirited, a form of punishment, and a means of perpetuating what NCLB claims to be correcting (Meier & Wood, 2004). Children and teachers in the official portrait are considered to be the source of the problem. Yet in our non-official portraits teachers and students contested official descriptions of them as not making Adequate Yearly Progress (AYP), being less than grade level proficient, and perpetuating chronic school failure. The students that compose counterportraits have been in school since NCLB was first implemented. The non-official portraits presented here challenge the prevailing (official) belief that they have never met the demands of official school success.

The Official Portrait

The official portrait of Mesa Vista Elementary School, the students, and their families is imbedded in the official portrait of the town as well as the state of New Mexico more broadly. Mesa Vista Elementary School is located in rural New Mexico in a township considered to have low population density, just over 1100 people per square mile. The school sits almost one mile above sea level in a ten square mile area. Its official portrait identifies the US/México border, drugs, gangs, languages other than English (i.e., predominantly Spanish but also including indigenous languages), poverty, and ties to México and Indian reservations as key problems that underpin the problem of scholastic failure. National, state and local level data came from reliable private and public sources, such as the Annie E. Casey Foundation (AECF, 2007) and U.S. Census Bureau (2008). Data is relevant to the time of the study in order to portray the reified view of students, teachers, the school and the official context. Some of the data presented are not cited in order to preserve the anonymity of students, teachers, and the school.

On a number of income measures, New Mexico is considered one of the poorest states in the United States. "In 2000, the poverty threshold for a family of two adults and two children [in New Mexico] was $17,463" (AECF, retrieved September 17, 2007). As recently as 2006, it was reported that 26% of New Mexico's children live at or below the federal poverty standard based on income. Only Louisiana and Mississippi rank lower. Similarly, New Mexico ranks 44th in terms of children living in extreme poverty—meaning their family's income is 50% or less of the federal poverty standard. More than 10% of K-12 students in New Mexico live with food insecurity, not knowing the source of their next meal.

On a variety of quality of life measures, New Mexico's children and youth are further considered at risk. In 2004, there were 28 child deaths per 100,000—ranking the state 41st in the nation; there were 88 teen deaths per 100,000—ranking the state 40th. Moreover, 41% of New Mexico's children live in families in which no parent has full-time, year-round employment—ranking the state 47th. Approximately 28% of children were born to mothers with less than 12 years of education—ranking the state 37th. In 2005, 17% of children age 17 and younger did not have health insurance—ranking the state 48th.

However, there have been increases in school age population in several semi-rural, semi-suburban communities largely due to the significantly lower prices for homes and the proximity to the state's largest city, where there are more jobs. Specifically, with respect to Mesa Vista Elementary's ambient community, the racial composition is: 58.7% Hispanic; 37.0% White Non-Hispanic; 27.6% other; 3.9% two or more races; 3.6% American Indian; and 1.2% Black. In the years 2001 - 2005, there were over 200 personal assaults in this township, making it among the highest percentage (per capita) for that crime in the state. In New Mexico, designations such as semi-rural, semi-suburban and majority minority (i.e., more non-Whites than Whites) often carry connotations like: *economically poor* (dependent on public assistance), *linguistically poor* (limited English proficiency), *socially poor* (aberrant [non-middle class] behavior), *and culturally poor* (uneducated and unable to value education).

In terms of student achievement, several measures from the National Assessment of Educational Progress (NAEP, 2005) point to official-designated problems, too. Twenty percent (20%) of fourth graders scored at or above the proficient level in reading. Similarly, 19% of eighth graders scored at or above proficient reading level. New Mexico ranked 41st in the nation with 61.5% of students graduating in four years. According to the United Health Foundation (2005, retrieved October 21, 2007)[1], the graduation rate had decreased 11.7% between 1990 - 2005.

The New Mexico Office of Education Accountability, the New Mexico Higher Education Department and the New Mexico Public Education Department track the state's percentage of high school graduates as they enter college (Winograd, Dasenbrock & García, 2008). This index underscores that although there was an increase of almost 16% in the number of students attending higher education institutions in 2007 compared to 2006, 50.1% of those students enrolled in remedial classes for numeracy and literacy. Additional results reveal that

- the percent of Native American students who take remedial courses has increased from 67% in 2000 to 68% in 2007;
- the percent of Hispanic students who take remedial courses has increased from 55% in 2000 to 58% in 2007;
- the percent of White students who take remedial courses has decreased from 36% in 2000 to 35% in 2007;
- the percent of Black students who take remedial courses has increased from 53% in 2000 to 54% in 2007;
- the percent of Asian students who take remedial courses has increased from 30% in 2000 35% in 2007; and
- New Mexico's public high schools (with more than ten students) ranged from [serving] 100% to 23% ... of their graduates who needed remediation. (p. 6)

The official portrait includes other images that reflect poor student achievement. New Mexico students fare much worse in preparedness for and performance in college than students in most other states in the US. According to the National Center for Public Policy and Higher Education, which has "evaluated the progress of the nation and all 50 states in providing Americans with education and training beyond high school through the bachelor's degree," (retrieved August 29, 2009 from http://measuringup2008.highereducation.org/), New Mexico's high school graduates' preparedness for college was graded a D- in 2008. Further, this same evaluation noted that eighth graders performed "very poorly in math, science, reading and writing." The state earned a B- in student participation in higher education—meaning that the state "does fairly well in providing college opportunities to its residents." However, a serious mitigating factor was noted: that college is prohibitively expensive for New Mexico youth. The evaluation awarded New Mexico an <F> in affordability. In other words, the opportunities to attend college exist, but few can afford to do so. Although New Mexico uses a lottery system to provide an undergraduate tuition award for eight consecutive semesters of full-time attendance (12 credit hours minimum) at a New Mexico public college or university to individuals who have graduated from a private or public high school, or have acquired a New Mexico General Educational Development certificate, the reality is that few can afford room and board costs. The state earned a D+ in terms of undergraduates completing their degree programs, noting that "only 42% of college students complete a bachelor's degree within six years," of which only 37% were Hispanic. Lastly, the evaluation noted that only 13% of the state's Hispanics have earned bachelor's degrees compared to 40% of the state's whites. This is "one of the largest gaps in the nation," and it represents a gradual increase since 2000. New Mexico remains well below the U.S. average in most areas. All these data point to one official conclusion: failure. Schools, children and youth and teachers are all officially considered at risk.

The district in which Mesa Vista Elementary is situated includes ten elementary, two middle and two high schools. There are also three "special" schools, such as the half-day family school that relies upon families to teach reading and language arts and a technical high school. There were 8,081 students enrolled in the district during the 2007-08 school year: 1,947 high school students, 1,446 middle school students and 4,688 elementary students. All of the students at Mesa Vista qualified for free and/or reduced breakfast and lunch programs. Mesa Vista Elementary had at least one, and sometimes two, uniformed police officers on campus. They did not carry guns.

Over twenty percent of the children at Mesa Vista Elementary are homeless.

A number of teachers refer to a large section of the Mesa Vista Elementary region as Little Juarez because so many of the families come from México, are economically poor and endure violence against and within their community.

Mesa Vista Elementary has never met Adequate Yearly Progress (AYP). The 2006 results showed that Mesa Vista Elementary did not reach the state goals in math (i.e., for the English language learner and special education subgroups) and reading (i.e., for the Hispanic, English language learner and special education subgroups). The district website lists all subgroups increasing 5% or more from 2005 to 2007. More specifically, all students and the subgroups of Hispanic, English language learner and Free/Reduced Lunch Program (FRLP) showed an equivalent improvement in math. In reading, Hispanic students increased five percent or more from the previous year's performance. Yet despite the fact that the subgroups may have improved by approximately five percent the school is not credited with meeting AYP because the gains were not sufficient enough to exceed the cut off line. Instead, in the popular press, one description of the school is presented: Mesa Vista Elementary students do not meet AYP.

Quite often, officially labeled *failing schools*, such as Mesa Vista Elementary, are highlighted as pipelines to social problems. The official portrait exploits these illustrations to suggest evidence of the pathology of underrepresented children and youth and the ineffectiveness of public education. Officializing these kinds of representations have an overwhelming influence even on teachers and students such that they come to believe gross generalizations made about them by those who do not know them and cannot see all that they actually accomplish. There is deference to the predominant point of view, the official propaganda and the daunting position to which they are relegated.

Realizing Something Definitely Needed to Be Different

In the summer of 2006, I presented a weeklong workshop—focusing on literacy strategies that are culturally responsive (Au, 1993) and reflect a critical perspective (Lewison, Flint & Van Sluys, 2002)—to approximately 75 fourth through sixth grade teachers from two rural districts in proximity to the university town in which I work. I started our work by explaining to the teachers that many believe that curriculum is something that can be composed away from a school site and delivered as a product to teachers—who then deliver it to children—in slick boxes containing books, workbooks, and worksheets to be used for teaching and assessing. Many of the teachers were surprised when I suggested that such kits were not curriculum, but were in fact other people's agendas for teachers and students they do not know. I further explained that curriculum needed to be something that unfolded as informed and thoughtful teacher-made decisions based on a teacher's knowledge of her students. Those decisions needed to include understanding and consideration of context: culture, experience, language, as well as official standards. Some of the teachers were shocked when I explained that curriculum is always, first and foremost, about relationships. It is the relational nature of curriculum that publishers deny as they sell prescriptions designed to standardize children and youth. They contended that this would be difficult for them to use in practice because their students needed so much help—they knew so little. I suggested that the children of New Mexico are not broken. They do not need any more help than children anywhere else in the US; they do not need to become exactly like one another. Rather, they are starved for honest relationships with teachers in which they can explore, inquire, challenge, and interrogate their worlds and the world around them. I further emphasized that when children engage in such work, they become reflective readers and writers and thoughtful citizens for a democracy. A curriculum developed through a relational process that honors students' and their teachers' identities while examining and questioning the world is both culturally responsive and critical. Teaching this way exceeds the state's standards, something many of the teachers worried about because the official portrait of their school called for strict links between official curriculum and test results.

The theme of our week together, working daily from 8:30 a.m. until 4:30 p.m., was honesty. Our work reflected serious scholarly activity, such as extensive reading, writing, discussion and presentation. "Tell your truths this week," I implored on our first day. "I will. You try to do it too, even if your truths are not the same as your colleagues and friends. Talk, think, and write from your hearts this week." We read together, wrote together, laughed together and cried together. We examined and questioned what happens in schools as we read critically acclaimed literature about racism, borders, Mexican connections, and Mexican art because these were reflective of their students' lives. During breaks, participants told me that they'd never considered teaching this way, and the focus on themselves as curriculum decision-makers both excited and threatened them. The thought of individual classrooms, especially those at the same grade levels, engaged in different activities, specifically reflective of the teachers' and students' talents, needs, and interests, challenged the institutional regularities (Sarason, 1972) and demands to which they had grown accustomed. Still, their curiosity was piqued about teaching differently, by honoring their students' and their own identities and subjectivities as well as developing relationships with each other.

At the conclusion of the week, a few of the teachers from Mesa Vista invited me to teach a graduate course at one of their schools in order to continue the process we had already begun. Because there were six different requests by teachers for the course to be taught at their school's sights, we settled on a central location in the district. Once the year started, however, two teachers at Mesa Vista Elementary self-identified as willing to further explore with their students how to make room for culturally responsive and critical literacy in their classrooms, pushing the limits of what was officially allowable. By self-identified, I mean that they had many questions and were sincerely willing to use instructional and planning time as spaces for real inquiry. They were passionate about having me participate with their students and them during some of those times. The remainder of their colleagues had lost the enthusiasm they shared in the summer workshop as they anticipated the pressures they would face in the classroom with the start of school drawing near. Being well aware of the many pressures teachers face, quite honestly, I was genuinely surprised that even two were moved sufficiently by the summer experience to want to continue with this kind of intensive, participatory work.

Mesa Vista Elementary is reminiscent of Goffman's (1961) "institutional display [in which] the displayed part of the institution is likely to be the new, up-to-date part..." (p.104). The main building of the school is a beautiful brick front with an overhanging and rather dramatic blue metal roof that seems to dissolve into the azure New Mexico sky. The school's name is in large silver letters above the doorway. Upon entering through two sets of glass and metal doors, a hallway opens to an indoor atrium with live plants and trees reaching to the ceiling. To the left are the principal's and nurse's offices, library, computer room, and cafeteria. The picture perfect front of the school almost feels contradicted by the large posters that display grade level performances on the statewide tests. Stretching outside from the main interior corridor are two parallel long lines of classroom pods constructed of corrugated metal. They have no internal hallway, but there is a concrete walkway with corrugated metal roof overhangs for each line of pods. Each pod consists of four classrooms around a small lobby, typically all of the same grade level. Each classroom has one window and two solid institutional green steel doors, one opening from the small lobby and the other leading to the playground. The window is about two feet high and wide and has an interior blind that can be raised or lowered. The rooms are not well heated or cooled. When the school year starts in August, the desert heat is still quite intense; classrooms are cool in the morning but quickly become uncomfortably hot as the unprotected building is overcome by the lingering summer sun. Just a few months later, as seasons turn to winter, the opposite is true; classrooms are cold in the morning as most of the students remain bundled in their coats. As the day warms slightly, the heating system overcompensates, and the rooms often reach temperatures of 80-85 degrees.

Patia Morales[2], a sixth grade teacher, Barbara Hopkins, a fifth grade teacher, and their students, welcomed me to their classrooms for the entire 2006 – 2007 school year. I visited once a week and spent about a half day in each classroom, which included literacy time. For the majority of literacy instruction, students had been placed into homogenous groups according to reading level—as determined by state and district mandated tests. To that end, Patia and Barbara were supposed to teach a basal reading program to groups of children that included some of their own students as well as students from the three other classes at each grade level. They were further mandated to follow scripts exactly as presented in the basal teacher manual. Teachers were to: read the story to the students, direct students to reread the story multiple times, ask the students comprehension questions, distribute skills' sheets, assign workbook pages, and administer regular and standardized tests. Reading time took 75-90 minutes every day. Patia complied because she believed that the district made an informed decision about a program that would help her students. Barbara tended towards challenging what was prescribed and often made more time to explore other literacy options, even to the point of telling her fifth grade colleagues that she would not follow the basal program some days. Given the complicated nature of this situation and the limited time available, we agreed to focus mostly on writing which did not have a prescribed curriculum and had been put on the back burner due to high stakes testing in reading and math.

The official portrait of Mesa Vista Elementary is bleak because of the generalizations drawn and demands made according to a punitive framework. The official portrait was the image that I carried in my mind as I initiated work with Patia, Barbara, and their students. Some teachers at the school echoed repeatedly certain elements of that portrait—especially the stereotypes about families in poverty not assuming agency in any way to change their lives. I continued to remind myself of that image even after I was invited to help Patia and Barbara rethink their practices and the assumptions and beliefs underlying them. Despite the weight of this image on my psyche, I was prepared to think with these teachers and their students about what literacy is for and to take actions with them on our new understandings. Of course, the issues we would face were embedded in larger struggles, such as district curriculum guidelines, state testing mandates and national funding regulations, and, of course, the larger social issues discussed earlier. Although we did not pretend we could simply change or overturn these demands, we were assertive about including alternative conceptualizations and compositions of literacy in classroom practice. We did not defer. Our work with students, drawing on their experiences, interests, needs, languages, cultures, and other relevant contexts, provided new areas of engagement and expressions of literacy, far exceeding state standards. The focus of our work then was not on meeting standards; rather, our aim was to explore teaching and learning possibilities when students and their teachers searched for and named truths that mattered to them, in their words, in their worlds, and in the words and worlds of their loved ones.

References

Annie E Casey Foundation. (2007). Retrieved on September 17, 2007 from http://www.aecf.org.
Au, K. (1993). *Literacy instruction in multicultural settings.* Belmont, CA: Wadsworth/Thompson Learning.
Geertz, C. (1973). *The interpretation of cultures.* New York: Basic Books.
Goffman, E. (1959). *The presentation of self in everyday life.* New York: Anchor Books.
Goffman, E. (1961). *Asylums: Essays on the social situations of mental patients and other inmates.* Chicago: Aldine.
Goodman, K. (2006). *The truth about DIBELS: What it is: What it does.* Portsmouth, NH: Heinemann.
Lawrence-Lightfoot, S. & Davis, J.D. (1997). *The art and science of portraiture.* San Francisco: Jossey-Bass.
Lewison, M., Flint, A.S., & Van Sluys, K. (2002). Taking on critical literacy: The journey of newcomers and novices. *Language Arts (79),* 5, 382-392. New York, New York: Palgrave.
Meier, D. & Wood, G. (2004). *Many children left behind: How the No Left Behind Act is damaging our children and our schools.* Boston: Beacon Press.
Moje, E. (2007). Developing socially just subject-matter instruction: A review of the literature on disciplinary literacy. In L. Parker (Ed.), *Review of research in education.* (pp. 1-44). Washington, DC: American Educational Research Association.
National Center for Public Policy and Higher Education. (2008). Retrieved from http://measuringup2008.highereducation.org/.
Rose, M. (2009) *Why School?* New York: The New Press.
Sarason, S. (1972). *The culture of the school and the problem of change.* Boston: Allyn and Bacon.
United Health Foundation (2005). *America's health ratings: A call to action for people and their communities.*
http://www.unitedhealthfoundation.com/shr2005/components/hsgrad.html (retrieved November 21, 2007).
US Census Bureau (2008). *Current population survey.* Washington DC: US Census Bureau. Retrieved August 29, 2008 from http://www.census.gov/cps/.
US Department of Education. (2001). Elementary and Secondary Education Act: Public Law PL 107-110, the *No Child Left Behind Act of 2001.* Retrieved
Winograd, P., Dasenbrock, R. & García, V. (2008). *Ready For College2008: An Annual Report On New Mexico High School Graduates Who Take Remedial Classes In New Mexico Colleges And Universities.* Santa Fe, New Mexico: Office of Education Accountability, Department of Finance and Administration.

Notes

[1] This foundation draws data from the National Center for Educational Statistics
[2] All names of teachers, children, and the school are pseudonyms.

CHAPTER SIX
ENCOUNTERING NEW DEMANDS—
COMPOSING NON-OFFICIAL PORTRAITS

Richard J. Meyer, University of New Mexico
With[1] Patia Morales, Barbara Hopkins and 5th and 6th grade students,
Mesa Vista Elementary School

In this essay, I portray the participatory work Patia, Barbara, the fifth and sixth graders and I accomplished together—featuring the students' writing as counter-portraits of the contexts of their literacy struggle and achievement. In this way we illustrate a bright image of them as competent and resourceful learners. We engaged the students' growing critical consciousness (Freire, 1970a) of themselves as writers of the world around them and their words to demonstrate multiple non-official portraits. Our work together was a forum speaking about and speaking back to the official portrait of the teachers, students and the school. Drawing upon Park's (as cited in Goffman, 1959) suggestion that, "everyone is always and everywhere more or less consciously playing a role...mask[ing] our truer self, the self we would like to be," (p. 19) we considered our work together and the contexts we inhabited to be the stage for our masquerade. We looked more closely at these contexts by making these more explicit. Moreover, we created a third space (Gutiérrez, Baquedano-Lopez and Turner, 1997) in which the official literacy curriculum was renegotiated in order to feature the students' lives, the people they loved, their homes and communities, their understandings and views of the world around them and their words for describing ignored realities of their contexts. Both teachers played crucial roles in the thinking and enacting of this work. The work of the two classes is blended in what follows.

Writing to Tell the Truth

On the first day of writing together, I presented *A Chicano Borderlander* (Martínez, 1994) to the sixth graders and told them that we'd discuss the poem with one guiding principle: they must tell the truth. They could decide how much of the truth to tell, but they needed to tell the truth. I challenged them to notice the differences in truths across individuals. And, I emphasized that we'd work to understand and respect all of these. We wanted many ideas.

In the poem, *A Chicano Borderlander*, Martínez discusses being from two countries (México and the US), two worlds, two languages, two cultures, and more.

> "What do you think of this poem?" I ask.
> "Read it again," one of the boys calls out.
> —I read it again. I don't know their names that well (yet) and voices seem to jump out.
> "I don't understand it," a girl calls out.
> "What's bilingual?" another asks.
> —I'm surprised at this question because most of the children are bilingual, yet they do not seem to have the metalinguistic awareness of what this means.
> "Yeah, and what's bicultural and binational?"
> —I think further about how most of these students share these contexts, too.

I give them the copies I was going to give the graduate class and read the poem again. I talk about the poem again, suggesting:

> "This is just what I think. It's not the right answer. There is no right answer. It's how I understand Oscar Martínez's truth about who he is and where he's from. You might think it's different. Do you? What do you think he means?"
> —I'm talking to fill the eerie silence, and demonstrate how to respond to a poem.

No response from the students; they wait patiently, looking intently at me. I explain a few of the terms in the poem and then talk about my own life in two worlds: a kid both Jewish and poor, as well as a kid who felt like he didn't understand things very much (i.e., my mother's sicknesses).

> "That's more than two worlds," someone calls out.
> "Yes," I laugh.
> —They do too. Some of them, anyway.
> "Any thoughts?" I ask.
> —As I'm waiting again, it feels like an eternity passes.
> "It's about us," comes a voice from the back of the room.
> "How?" I ask.
> "We live in two worlds and one is in English and one is in Spanish. "
> "Who else?" I ask.

Some others talk, making references to lines in the poem that they're rereading. I wait.

"I like the part about being Mexican and being American," one of the girls says. "Read that line," I say.

She reads it aloud. More silence. I continue to wait.

"How come you chose that line?" I ask.

But questions may be considered punishment for children in school, something I remember as I realize all the asking I'm doing. Authority figures ask things like, "Why did you do that?" or "Can't you be quiet?" Questions don't always demand answers and when they do many children fall into recitation scripts in which they expect there to be one right answer (Mehan, 1982). So I continue to wait.

One of the boys talks about being between two countries, still having family in México and visiting them when he can. A few others tell briefly about crossing the border at or near El Paso. Their teacher, Patia, offered:

"Why do people have to call us Hispanic or Chicana? I'm not a Chicana. I'm a Mexican American. Why is it such a big deal? Why is it so difficult to call me that?"

Patia has now engaged with the students, questioning what she is called by others, but not necessarily what she calls herself, and trying to make sense of it.

"Any thoughts about what your teacher just read?" I ask.

Silence. I suggest that we use the poem as a starting point for our own writing. The children immediately moan and complain about writing.

"You don't have to write," I say and they all look at me. "You *get* to write. You have something to say about who you are and you get to write it. So write it."

What follows is what a few of the students wrote in about fifteen minutes. For most, it was the first time queries about their first language, home culture, and personal and family issues were committed to paper and shared voluntarily in public. *Vianca* wrote about a longstanding sadness she feels:

I'm sad because the Americans call us, the Mexicans, all kinds of names and I'm sad too because my family fights a lot and I'm sad too because I always hear my friends talking about their dad and I don't have a dad.

Verdad sinks into her paper with intensity and composes her frustration with power and getting in trouble for standing up for herself:

I hate when I get in trouble at school. I don't like when they made some game of Mexicans that are crossing the border and they shoot people. This is what happened to me at school, in [another town] one day: We were playing soccer and some kids just started to call us stupid Mexicans. We got mad. They told us bad words and other stuff. D——, a friend of mine, even gave a black eye to some kids named.... Just for calling us stupid Mexicans. We got in trouble and they did, too. We were really mad at them.

Stories of aggravation, sadness, and worry abound, as do stories about family here and in México, about the border and about crossing back and forth to be together again. *Esperanza* writes:

> When my mom went to México, she took my little brothers. And did not take my sister or me. When she was coming, they caught her and they called my dad. She was in jail. They wanted a lot of money to let her go. They let her go and my uncle went for my brothers. At the end, they gave the papers to my mom. Now she could go to México. That was very happy.

Lorenzo is aware that there are official rules about who gets to cross the US/México, and that lies are told in order to get the least desirable work done.

> I feel that it's not fair that they don't let the Mexicans across the border. They're the ones that do all the work here, like building houses and everything like that.

Carlos also understands what it means to feel like a perpetual outsider and unwanted guest as he writes quite succinctly,

> We are stuck in a place with hate.

For me their words resonated with the passionate understanding that writers like Gloria Anzaldúa (1999) expressed as she wrote about living in contested contexts:

> I want the freedom to carve and chisel my own face, to staunch the bleeding with ashes, to fashion my own gods out of entrails. And if going home is denied me then I will have to stand and claim my space, making a new culture—una cultura mestiza—with my own lumber, my own bricks and mortar and my own feminist architecture. (p. 44)

In our first writing session together, the students, their teacher, and I began to redesign the space for literacy in the classroom, moving from one dominated by others' demands to one that opened up room for composing literacy from the students' lived experiences, in their voices and with unequivocal recognition that can read, respond to and write sophisticated texts. I do not mean, by any measure, to romanticize this work. It did not go smoothly. There was a great deal of apprehension about committing ideas to paper and an equal amount of shying away from sharing. I struggled with their silences, and wondered how we were going to continue. I contemplated whether I was witness to the age-old strategy, students learn in school, of remaining silent in order to draw out the single right answer expected by the teacher—often provided by the teacher. I was distressed with their hesitations. I filled the silences with my questions but eventually realized that my discomfort was both temporary and mine alone. My biggest challenge at this point—by making this demand for a different curriculum and for a different approach to teaching and learning—was to convince them that my ideas were not the only worthwhile ideas and their ideas could be legitimate even if different than mine. They were more accustomed to school as a forum for certitude, in which learning almost always involved exercises of modeling and practicing right from wrong.

Although the oral discussion of the poem was awkward and fragile, the students' writing provided a way for them to further explore which words to use in order to be clear and explicit. In the quiet spaces into which they withdrew to write, always with the option of not sharing, they were willing to take –new-to-school risks. We ran out of time before we could read what they had written that day. In Barbara's classroom, the students began writing autobiographies, rather than use the poem. Barbara wanted them to focus on themselves, with the ultimate goal of writing a biography of someone they love. We then went on, in subsequent weeks, learning to design interview questions, which they asked each other, eventually writing biographies of each other.

The following week, I returned to the sixth grade with typed copies of their writing (this allowed me time to read more deliberately and respectfully). Some students read theirs and others allowed me to read their pieces aloud. I suggested to them that we'd broken a school rule. Most of them looked at me anxiously wondering; but, a few called out demanding to know which school rule it was. I said,

"We told the truth at school."
—I told truths, too, I thought to myself.

I had to invest honestly with my truths. I told them about my father's violent temper and my fears of my mother dying during a succession of bouts with cancer and other diseases. I explained that I never told my real truths at school. I never shared my fears, worries, sorrows, joys, or surprises.

The rule we'd broken had never been written anywhere. Nonetheless, we all knew it was true. I explained to both classrooms that during our writing time together, the truth mattered more than that rule because it was a non-official rule that demanded we break the unwritten one so that we could genuinely learn. Our struggle was to tell our truths because these mattered: Truths defined us, framed the choices we made about what to do everyday and even shaped who we were and would become. Our truths led to authentic demands we would place on our literacy activity. In Barbara's classroom, the fifth graders worked to tell their truths in autobiographies; they learned to solicit truth from others in writing biographies. *Consuelo* wrote:

The Giving One
I see my mom
with curly hair
wishing to get her papers
and never giving up
and as I hear her say,
"Se buena [be good],
Ayudame a limpiar [help me to clean],
Y haz la tarea [do your homework]."

as I hear inside her head
that she will give
love and attention
to her children and husband
Never gives up learning English
Never gives up teaching her children to do good
Never gives up getting her papers
Never gives up opportunities to get a job.

Naming and Sharing Personal Truths

The next time I visited the sixth grade classroom, I introduced GE Lyon's poem *Where I'm From* (reprinted in Christensen, 2000) as the point of origin for discussion and writing. I once again presented the students with the idea of telling their truths. Lyon's poem is a wonderful mixture of things that fifth and sixth graders could understand (e.g., the sweetness of fudge, dirt under a porch, shady trees, and the smell of strong coffee) and things they struggled to understand (e.g., Billie's Branch, carbon-tetrachloride, forsythia, auger, and Imogene and Alafair). They moaned about the parts that made no sense to them.

> "What do you understand?" I asked.
> "It's about a girl...you said George is a girl."
> "She is a woman," I restate.
> "That's not a girl's name."
> "What *do* you understand?" I request, again.
> "She ate dirt," someone yells out—and then a round of laughter.
> "Yeah, what's that all about? Why'd she do that?" I ask.

Silence.

> "Well, we don't know," I answer my own question. "It doesn't say. She didn't tell us why. She just said that she did it. The important thing is that it's a memory, something she remembers, something that tells her who she is and she is telling us. She's letting us know, 'Look, I ate some dirt'."

More silence.

> "What else do you get...do you understand in the poem?" I continue.

The answers start to come forward as the children read lines or parts of lines to the whole class.

> "She had a back porch."
> "The dirt tasted like beets."
> "She made a lamb at Sunday school, and her grandfather lost a finger—but we don't knowwhat an auger is."
> "There were pictures under her bed in an old dress box."

I point to the last three lines and say,

> "Look, look at the bottom. The third to last line says, 'I am from these moments.' I wish she just ended the poem there. I get all the stuff you just told me about dirt and a finger and all that. That is where she's from. That's what happened in her life. It's all real and it all makes sense. Even though there are some words you may not know and I may not know, I still get the idea of the poem. But now she writes, 'snapped before I budded—leaf-fallen from the family tree.' What does that mean?" I urge.

Silence. So I read those last two lines again.

> "She left her family," someone volunteers.
> "What else?" I continue.
> "She left her family," another one says.

The repetition of a peer's response was common when we started our work together. It seemed as though the students assumed that naming one right answer was sufficient to appease the teacher—me, in this case—and repeating what was said was a way of suggesting that the answer had been provided so we could move on. They were surprised when I asked, "What else?" disrupting the typical script of a classroom lesson by calling for more than one response to satisfy the teacher and complete the exercise.

My goal was not to end, but to begin, discuss, think, rethink, and revise, and then think again. My ultimate desire was focused on writing and sharing that writing. I was trying to teach the students that their personal truths were the stuff of what we were doing, and, further, that those truths could be tentative.

> "I heard that ('she left her family') the first time," I say, "but I'm not sure that is the only explanation. It can mean more than one thing. There's no right answer. We have to sort of guess."
> "Maybe she got thrown out of her family," comes a voice from a typically quiet student who always sits the back of the room.
> "Maybe," I acknowledge but also question. "Like maybe there was a fight or," I continued.
> "She ran away with a boyfriend," someone completes my sentence and others laugh.
> "I know," I say. "Any of those are good ideas."
> "Snapped," says one child. "'*Snapped* [exaggerating the word] before I budded,' means someone took her picture."
> "Oh, like with a camera," I say. "What else?"
> "I think she may have died," comes a hesitant voice.
> "She could have died," I agree. "So she is off the family tree because she died?"
> "But who wrote the poem, if she died?" someone challenges.
> "I have no idea. What do you think?" I ask.
> "Someone is writing like they are her, like she died but then they tell her story," someone else suggests.
> "There are a lot of ideas, aren't there?" I ask.
> "What's the right one?" asks one of the students.

"I have no idea. I'm not even sure if we did or didn't say the one that was on the poet's mind when she wrote it. It's for us to read and think about. And it's for us to wonder about where we came from, too."
—I'm encouraged by their fluid and sophisticated thinking.

We were, for that moment, transacting with the poem (Rosenblatt, 1978), as each volunteer offered something different to explain the lines. Each contributor was drawing upon his or her experiences, not just with school, but with life, to create a meaning for the poem that was theirs. Still, the slow-in-coming explanations were bounded by the social realities of the setting. They'd learned that school is the search for the one known answer (Mehan, 1982) and that the answer must fit not only the teacher-demanded parameters, but also the social fabric of their relationships with each other (Lewis, 2001). This classroom had norms, like any other community of practice (Holland, Skinner, Lachicotte, & Cain, 1998). The remarkable thing about this grand conversation (Peterson & Eeds, 1990) was that the students were challenging the imposed silence (Fine, 1996) that the official curriculum demanded by limiting the form, time and spaces for real discussion.

"So we have to write one?" asks one of the students.
"You will *get* to write one." I explain.

But first I present poems from other sixth graders that live in similar economically difficult situations (Filbrandt, 1999). These poems are truthful, about gangs, violence, drugs, language, homelands, and more. One of Filbrandt's students writes about living in a car when her family had no other place to live. Another writes about a leaky roof and the stains left on the ceiling following a rainstorm. Other pieces also seem to mirror the lives of many of the students in these classes. They are awestruck by the work of children they have never met. As the lives of these two groups resonate, the conversation deepens, subsides, and then pauses, I suggest that they write their own poems.

Mercedes' poem moves from food to pain to the realities of housecleaning to being cared for.

Where I'm From
I'm from the tamales and Mexican food
I'm from the people who get hurt every day.
I'm the girl who helps my mom clean the house every day.
I'm from the people who take care of me every day.

Miguel's piece highlighted more ordinary things, like sports and cooking, as well as uncommon—and far from officially sanctioned—activities such as selling drugs, crossing the border, and parents expressing anger.

I Come From
I come from playing sports
I come from an immigrant family
I come from my mom's tired eyes
I come from people selling drugs

I come from not choosing to do or sell drugs
I come from my mom crossing the border
I come from my mom making food for us
I come from horse racing, rooster and dog fighting
I come from leaks in my house
I come from education
I come from my family
I come from feeding my pets every day
I come from a lost little puppy
I come from a Mexican culture
I come from a paper holding my thoughts
I come from my parents getting mad at each other
That's where I come from.

Vianca is one of many children whose biological father is not present, leaving her mom depressed and the entire family vulnerable. Stress within the family is exhibited through things like fighting about money and struggling to overcome feelings of abandonment.

Where I Am From
I am from my family
that's trying to give me a good life.
I'm from a family
that is trying not to fight a lot.
I'm from a family
that is not poor and not rich.
I'm from a dad
that doesn't care of his family.
I'm from a mom
that's trying to be happy, not sad.

Father sometimes self-medicates to alleviate the pain they feel. Yet *Juliana* reflects her resolve to live with hope and strength in order to make better choices for herself and her family.

I come from a drunk dad.
I come from arguing with my mom everyday.
I come from the neighborhood, the
one that smokes and drinks and does
bad things.
I come from strong enough
to do better choices than that.

Juliana's process for writing this piece influenced the entire class, her teacher and me in unexpected but much needed ways. She'd written the first line of the poem and then wrapped her arms around the paper and put her head inside the cave she'd created. I pulled a chair beside her and the boy across from her told me that she was crying. I ask,

"Are you okay?" knowing that she's not.

She raises her head and looks at me, seeming to ask for forgiveness for having written only one line, the first line of the piece above.

"This is all I did," she says.
"That's okay," I reply. "Writing takes time and sometimes it takes tears."

The class is silent, which is rare, and all eyes are on Juliana and me. I ask,

"Do you want to read it?"

Juliana reads,

"I am from a drunk dad."
"It's true," the boy across from Juliana volunteers. "I see him around. He drinks a lot."

Juliana looks at me and I say, as others listen,

"You're doing really important work. You're writing your truth. When you're ready, you might write more."

Then I turn to the entire class, looking around as I say,

"One of your friends cried when she wrote. That is one way to know it's a real truth. We know it's from her heart because of her tears. That's one way to tell. I hope you'll all write from your hearts."

Over the course of the year, other students cried about death, material losses, ruined relationships, and unforgettable experiences. We laughed at some things that were truly funny; we also got impatient from time to time as we were learning to accept the spectrum of feelings we shared with each other—feelings of anger, boredom, curiosity, excitement, frustration, guilt, loneliness, shame, and surprise. Ramona's pride in her father's return from the war in Iraq led the fifth graders in Barbara's classroom to shift from self to others, as *Ramona* did when she wrote:

Dad
When most people think of my dad
They think army man
When I think of my dad I think
Dad, who helps and loves me
So yes he is an army man but
He's much more too
He's my brown hair brown eyed
Dad
He's my adoring, loving
Dad

He's my funny, smart
Dad
So don't only think army man also think
Dad.

Patia, Barbara, and I worked to confirm true regard for these feelings as part of the struggle to write with truthfulness. Sometimes Patia would panic about the slow pace of the work and my insistence to allow students, like Juliana, to ponder the one line or few words they had written. Yet Patia also noticed how she would cry at times when she wrote about similar issues in her life.

The demands to write truthfully, to share our writing and to accept each other's written truths would bracket the official demands for these brief periods of time. For example, *Corazon* knows that gangs disrupt families. Despite this realization, she finds herself left with the feeling that she is in the middle of constant conflict between loving her family and wishing she could change choices already made. She yearns for that place in her mind that she as a 'little girl' inhabits.

Where I'm From
I'm from making my mom proud of my grades,
I'm from my brother joining gangs and calling other people family,
Being thankful of his Westside homies,
I'm from my 2 families fighting against each other,
And from me being in the middle of those familie
And not being able to do nothing about their conflict,
I'm also from being the little girl
Of both families.

Verdad is well aware of the choice to remain silent, to become an observer of what happens around her, knowing that it has darkened her soul. Yet she remains proud of her roots.

I Come From
I come from my mom's dark eyes
I come from a Mexican family that crossed the border to survive
I come from my dark soul
I come from a immigrant family
I come from my dark silence
I come from my parents fighting because of my progress report
I come from my sister running away because of my parents fighting
I come from a Mexican family and I'm proud.

Jesus suffers from his brother's choices and is told to learn from those choices. But he leaves me wondering how he can choose if he does not know the essence of other options.

I am from gang signs growing up in a neighborhood with people who don't care who you are if you say something you might get jumped. One memory I remember is when my big brother got shot because he had a gun. The new one he got is more smaller. Going with him in his low-rider that has the front windshield broken by a crack head who wasn't in a good mood. At least my brother tells me he will always be there for me telling me to not live like this and not to ever do what he does, never to have a gun like he does. He also says to never sell or do drugs. He said to work for what I want. He also says if I want something bad enough, I will get it. He said if he can go back in time he would change everything. Me and my brother are closer than ever. We stick together. We both grew up without dads. My brother taught me what he knew and what he is learning. This life is hard and I'm trying to not live it. My brother said by seeing all this and not wanting to live it, will help me not live this life. I'm from pasole, quesadillas, enchiladas, and chili. I could go on forever but I don't have the time.

We wrote every Friday, deepening our understanding of ourselves, each other, our families, the community around us and the very real demands of everyday life we all face. The importance of self and the understanding of the many selves, or our subjectivities, that one may compose became central to our work. For the first time in their school lives, the children themselves were at the center of their learning; they were the subject.

We ventured into the darkness that *Verdad* discussed as I asked the children about the meaning of darkness following the reading of Sonia Manriquez's, *Dark Waters* (Ochoa, Franco, & Gourdine, 2003). Such emotionality is unarguably ignored the vast majority of the time in school. *Verdad's* familiarity with the idea of darkness found a space to express itself as she wrote:

Dark Eyes
When I see into
my mom's eyes I
see darkness
I see understanding
in the steaming room
making food
for my sister and me
as rivers of
tears come down her cheeks
fall down
her face that's when we realized
we are alone.

Vianca's use of the word *passed* in the next poem is an interesting, though I am not convinced intentional, play on words, suggesting the past as well as someone passing (i.e., dying).

Dark Passed
When I think
about my passed
I remember of
my grandfather
He used to
play with me
and take me
to the park
He used to

make me laugh
I know I'm alone.

Isaac's darkness is rooted in the reality and finality of death from a gang shooting.

Dark Home
When I look inside my
home.
I see darkness of my uncle
not being there
I open the door I feel my
uncle
but I open my eyes and I
realize no one is there.
that's when I realize
I will never see him again.

Several of the students know about loss as a quarter of them raised their hands when I asked who had family members killed by gangs. By January, these writings and the concomitant conversations led to our study of the community as the children interviewed loved ones about their lives, their immigration stories, and more. These biographical pieces led to more conversations as photographs, interviews, writing and sharing writing opened up new spaces for truth telling and the interrogation of their lives and the world around them. In one interview, for instance, Carlos learned about his father's immigration to the US from México:

I was born in Chihuahua, México. As a young boy, it has always been work since I was in elementary school. I believe I started working when I was seven years old. I would go to school and then I would go to work. Then I went to middle school and I had to pay each month and for books. I finished the second year of middle school, then I didn't want to return to school. People started to go to the US. They said that in the US you got a lot of money and that it was easy. Pure lies. (Translation excerpt from Carlos' interview with his dad.)

The students began to understand much of the disappointment they and their parents faced, and that, of course, there were no simple solutions. A number of them continued to suggest that if they worked hard enough, prayed long enough, or dreamed often enough, the hopes that they held for the US would be realized. Others proclaimed with sheer certainty that they were "stuck in a place with hate" that getting a better life was "pure lies."

The theme of *transitions* saturated our work during the year as the young writers consistently wrote about changes in their lives. As the year wound down, I asked them to write in the frame "I used to ..., but now ...," in which they could summarize changes in their lives over time. When they completed these brief pieces, I put them into a slideshow on the computer, but neglected to put their names on their slides. This mistake turned out to be an advantage because preserving anonymity let us discuss their writing without being accusatory, defensive, or in any other way resistant to sharing ideas. The excerpt below is an illustration of this theme across a number of students' writing. For the most part, the transitions reflected a change in disposition and outlook— from presence to absence, from happiness to sadness:

> *I used to have a dad, but now I don't.*
> *I used to have a grandfather, but now I don't.*
> *I used to have a little dog, but now I don't.*
> *I used to have curiosity of what the world was like, but now I don't.*
> *I used to think I had powers that would one day come to me, but now I know it's impossible.*
> *I used to think that other people tried to help you because they were trying to be nice, but now I know the truth.*
> *I used to think that life was easy, but now I know it's hard.*
> *I used to believe in Santa Claus, but now I know it was our parents.*
> *I used to think everyone was peaceful, but now I know that some people are violent.*
> *I used to have an uncle, but he's gone forever.*
> *I used to think all cool, but now I don't.*
> *I used to talk back to my mom, but now I don't 'cause it's disrespect.*
> *I used to have a best friend, but now I know there are no best friends.*
> *I used to not get in trouble, but now I get in trouble.*
> *I used to not fight, but now I fight.*
> *I used to sleep in my room, but now I don't sleep in my room.*
> *I used to think that life would never end, but now I know.*
> *I used to believe in trust, but now I don't.*
> *I used to want peace, but now I know violence makes the world go 'round.*
> *I used to think he was the worst uncle,*
> *but now I know he was like that because he cared about me.*

About a week later, I asked that they tell the story behind one or more of the changes they'd written about in the brief pieces. Thematically, most of the children wrote about transitions they had to make with people who mattered dearly to them and the pain they experienced when their relationships were threatened. The following are a sampling of their elaborations (i.e., stories behind the transitions). The first line of each piece is from their original list; after choosing and copying that line onto a new piece of paper, they wrote their elaborations.

> *I used to have a family, but now I don't.*
> *The whole story behind this is talking about my life of how where I was five years old my mom had a really bad argument and moved. Our family was torn apart. Now that I'm 12, I don't have any trust in my dad at all. I try to but I can't. Sometimes I'm actually scared to talk to him because for some reason he hates my mom. And sometimes doesn't stop [talking] bad about her that's why I used to have a family but now I don't. —Corazón*

> *I used to want peace, but now I know violence makes the world go 'round.*
> *The story behind this one is that I would have not learned what drugs are or even what they looked like. I wouldn't have had a clue about who was probably bad just by looking at them. People say not to judge a book by it color but that's the first way I judge all persons. If there was peace on earth, cops would not have a job. Also, the life cycle has to have violence. It's what makes the earth go 'round. Another thing I hate to see is when two people act like if they like each other, but then again if there was peace on earth, maybe I would have met my dad. —Jesús*

I used to think all cool, but now I don't.
Because my brother always tells me that I shouldn't because one of these days someone is going to kick your butt and almost kill you. —Lorenzo

I used to have a favorite uncle, but now I don't.
Because I don't have a favorite uncle. The story is that I don't have a favorite uncle is because they killed him. They killed him because he didn't pay those people some money. So they decided to kill my uncle. Now my uncle is in heaven where he is supposed to be. —Verdad

Some of these elaborations reflect a topic the individual wrote about often in our work together. For example, Verdad wrote repeatedly about her uncle being "where he is supposed to be" or "in a better place." At the end of our project, she also wrote a biography about him that was informed by interviews she did with other family members as well as her recollections of him. She emphasized how he came to the US to find a better place, but it was far from what he expected. A similar transition was evident in many of her peer's writing. They seemed to be pointing out their growing critical awareness of the depth and extent of struggled involved in getting to the US and surviving here. Verdad further learned from others and came to understand that her uncle's to death was the change that was truly best for him. She missed him and carried with her a sequestered rage about his struggles and losing him. She let some of that leak into her writing, as did her class peers once they began to feel safe enough to respond to the internal demands they felt.

For all of these children, critical reflection on the themes of violence, gangs, borders, families, and economic crises in their lived experiences would continue long after our project. In August, just before the new school, Verdad's father committed suicide in her family's home. Her younger brother found their dad after he had shot himself. Other quieter and seemingly less dramatic signifiers of failure continued to predominate as well: homelessness, food shortages, changing family constellations, drug use, prostitution, and lack of money to pay for hot water, heating and cooling in the trailers in which they lived. Despite living with these constant stressors, the fifth and sixth graders wrote boldly, creatively and seemingly fearlessly about the truths of their realities. As these writings were shared and discussed over and over again, the children and their teachers began to re-examine the official portrait they had taken for granted—that they were failures—and instead they appropriated a new image of their identities, solidarity as a community of learners and success, built across their recent experiences in this project. I read many pieces to them by Chicana and Chicano writers in which those writers explained the strength-building inherent in naming and sharing all kinds of experiences, including both the realities for people who were never able to change their circumstances and the different realities for those who did.

References

Anzaldúa, G. (1999). *Borderlands/La Frontera: The new mestiza* (3rd edition). San Francisco: Aunt Lute Books.

Christensen, L. (2000). *Reading, writing, and rising up: Teaching about social justice and the power of the written word.* Milwaukee: Rethinking Schools.

Filbrandt, T. (1999). Poetry and transformation. *Primary Voices 8*(2), 11-18.

Fine, M. (1996). Silencing in Public Schools. In *Language development: A reader for teachers*, B. Power & R. Hubbard (Eds.). (pp. 243-254).Englewood Cliffs, NJ: Merrill/Prentice Hall.

Freire, P. (1970). The adult literacy process as cultural action for freedom. *Harvard Educational Review, 40* (2), 205-225.

Goffman, E. (1959). *The presentation of self in everyday life.* New York: Anchor Books.

Gutiérrez, K., Baquedano-Lopez, P. & Turner, M.G. (1997). Putting language back into language arts: *When the radical middle meets the third space. Language Arts 74*(5), 368-378.

Holland, D., Skinner, D., Lachicotte, W. & Cain, C. (1998). *Identity and agency in cultural worlds.* Cambridge, MA: Harvard University Press.

Lewis, C. (2001). *Literacy practices as social acts: Power, status, and cultural norms in the classroom.* Mahwah, NJ: Erlbaum.

Martínez, O. (1994). 'Chicano Borderlander' in *Border people: Life and society in the U.S.-México Borderlands* (pp. 116-117). Tucson: University of Arizona Press.

Mehan, H. (1982). The structure of classroom events and their consequences for student performance. In P. Gilmore & A. Glatthorn (Eds.), *Children in and out of school: Ethnography and education*, (pp. 59-87). Washington, D.C.: Center for Applied Linguistics.

Ochoa, A., Franco, B., & Gourdine, T. (2003). *Night is gone, day is still coming: Stories and poems by American Indian teens and young adults.* Cambridge, MA: Candlewick Press.

Ohanian, S. (1999). *One size fits few: The folly of educational standards.* Portsmouth, NH: Heinemann.

Peterson, R. & Eeds, M. (1990). *Grand conversations: Literature groups in action.* Ontario, Canada: Scholastic.

Rosenblatt, L. (1978). *The reader, the text, the poem: The transactional theory of the literary work.* Carbondale: Southern Illinois University Press.

Notes

[1] All names, including the teachers' and that of the school, are pseudonyms.

CHAPTER SEVEN
ACTING UPON, WITH, AND FOR LITERACY

Richard J. Meyer, University of New Mexico
With Patia Morales, Barbara Hopkins and 5th and 6th grade students,
Mesa Vista Elementary School

Our writing work went deeper and deeper into truths as our time together meandered towards the end of the school year. Patia, the sixth grade teacher, seemed more relaxed once the state tests were administered, but her angst was renewed when she learned about another set of tests yet to be taken. The pressure on both teachers was intense, but Barbara was more inclined to focus on the children's work and worry less about their performance on tests. Barbara also learned to use the project as a shield, explaining to her colleagues that her class needed to go in different directions. Both teachers and I saw our roles as supporting the students in learning about and committing to paper and digital formats their stories and the stories of loved ones. By the end of the year, the students had multiple pieces—mostly poems—about themselves and at least one in-depth narrative piece about a loved one. The work seemed to generate its own importance and inertia, particularly when the students wrote about loved ones. The extension into writing others' stories (i.e., individuals, typically family members, who were not in school) evolved fairly naturally as the children mentioned these people in their own narratives and asked questions of each other about their families. Demands to know more led to further inquiry.

A particularly important part of this process was this turn in their writing to the stories of loved ones. We lent digital voice recorders and cameras to students. They practiced interview strategies with each other in preparation for collecting stories and photo-observation techniques to add dimension and perspective to their work. The entire process took weeks. Three excerpts from students' writing about loved ones are presented here to highlight the development of their writing craft and skill. These pieces averaged ten pages in length each and included photos, direct quotes, and diverse narratives reflecting many truths.

Miguel wrote about his mother's compassion and conviction:

> My mom was born in a small village called El Azulillo, Jalisco, México. She came to the U.S.A. to work so she could help her parents because they were very poor. The people there were all very poor. She said, "They needed me to help them". … Her first job was cleaning offices. Then she meets her husband and she stopped working. She met her husband in Phoenix; she lived with her brother in the same apartment complex where they met, and then got married. She didn't want to live in México because she wanted to work over here. She came to live with her brothers and her sister-in-law in the United States.

Verdad wrote about her uncle's legacy, one of striving toward a goal with unwavering focus and sharing his joy in the midst of overwhelming hardship:

> My uncle came to the United States to work, to live a better life. The first job that my uncle had was working in a restaurant. He worked washing dishes for a couple of months. Later he worked in a factory that made paper. He stayed there for a couple of years because he liked that job and they paid him much more than his first job. Also, he made a lot of friends.… The experience that my uncle had was that coming to the USA is not an easy thing because there's various obstacles on the road. Like for example when he crossed the Rio [River] it was a very sad experience because the current almost took him. But at the end, he was able to cross fine.

Vianca, like most of the other children, learned about events that occurred when she was very young, or possibly before she was born. She was one of many children who learned interview strategies in English, composed questions in English, and then found she needed to translate the questions to Spanish in order to conduct the interviews and collect extensive narratives. Subsequently, she translated her findings into English so that audiences in venues beyond the school could understand her work. *Vianca* wrote about her grandmother, who is her guardian, and how she made her way to the US.

> She came to the United States to be with her children. Her children came illegally in 1990. She said that when they came to the US there were four adults and one girl, who was me. It took us a month to pass the border through the desert. We were detained by immigration two times. We were coming in a truck. She told me that the first two times that we were detained by immigration were when we were crossing the border. The third time we passed (entered) fine into the US.

The completed pieces were further translated into computer slide shows and then printed out and bound so that the students and their families would have evidence of the results of their labors.

The children learned of the commitments their families had to a 'better life,' something families imagined existed beyond the Mexican border. They learned about their families' struggles and, for many, they began to talk of their family members as heroes. Estevan interviewed his dad. The following excerpt provides an illustration of the tenor of the interviews that the children conducted as precursors to their writing.

Estevan: "What about your family?"
Javier: "I want everybody in the family to never be without food."
Estevan: "Is that all your work jobs?"
Javier: "I've always done carpet, laid carpet."
Estevan: "After he [your second son] was born, how did you feel?"
Javier: "I was happy. I have two sons and a wife."
Estevan: "Are you still doing carpet?"
Javier: "Yes, I'm gonna die doing carpet because that's the only thing I know how to do. That's the only thing I know how to do. [He says this twice.]"

Our writing and thinking time together grew in intensity and dedication; the moment the children saw me step into the school, they immediately approached me, reported the status of their work and requested that we start work on the writing as soon as I could get to the classroom. As the children seemed to change—growing and writing themselves into newer understandings of themselves and others in their lives—we decided that the work demanded a greater audience. It was with that newly realized awareness—of the importance of a wider audience—that the idea of counterportraits emerged. I considered that although what was painted into the minds of others might be powerfully inscribed, it might be open to revision. These fifth and sixth graders could play a role in making those revisions, changing the official portrait of failure to one of a struggle against failure and the themes of poverty, gangs, etc., that suggest and often underpin it. Over a series of class meetings, I suggested to the students and their teachers that we share our learning with a wider audience so that others might know these children and their contexts for who they truly are. Not surprisingly, I was again met with resistance, but as the opportunities became imaginable, the children seemed more willing—even excited—to share their work.

I arranged for the children to present their writing to 100 preservice teachers at the University of New Mexico as part of a yearly undergraduate conference. Together the children gave the keynote address. They also met in small groups with the soon-to-be teachers and watched in wonder as these adults cried, laughed, and listened in amazement to the writing the children had done during the year. I explained that the children were from a school that never met AYP, but that the children's progress as writers was dramatic, important, and positive. They would carry this success with them in the years ahead as they continued in school and became active, responsible citizens in their communities. They knew how to make their voices heard—their demands would indeed become visible. The future teachers gained insights into teaching and learning by hearing stories that no methods class had yet featured and no basal program allowed. These non-official portraits, then, provided generative themes for the fifth and sixth graders, their teachers, me and pre-service teachers, which engaged us all—in different ways—in transforming understandings and potentially changing actions. This is the essence of Freire's (1970) conscientization—consciousness raising with the ultimate goal of action for a more just and decent democracy.

It was at this meeting between fifth and sixth grade students and future teachers that the possibilities for counterportraiture became somewhat evident. The fifth and sixth graders had changed through the writing, becoming more conscious about the need and purpose for their work. Witnessing the influence of their work on such a large audience gave the children a renewed sense of the value of their experience, their expertise, what they had to say in writing, and why it matters. As we left the conference, the children talked about adults crying and laughing while listening to their words with a level of intensity and wonder that caught their teachers and me by surprise. Probably only a few, if any, expected the kind of emotional engagement that the pre-service teachers reflected. This experience with representing their literacy achievement to outsiders confirmed the power of their context, experiences and writing. It shifted the demands literacy had in their lives for a few moments as their literacy was placed in a position of authority.

Later that same afternoon, the children worked with an award winning poetry slam team—a group of poets who, in several respects, looked and sounded much like the children. The poets performed and then invited the children to write and perform as well. The poets critiqued the children's work, but mostly they shared their respect for the intensity and truthfulness of the writing. They read some of what the children had presented earlier in the day and they spoke with the children about the strengths they saw in their writing. The children had two powerfully confirming moments in one day—moments during which their counterportraits were acknowledged, their voices were heard, and their understanding of the possibilities for renewing their perspectives of themselves and their contexts were honored by others.

When I next met with the children, I attempted to celebrate with them what we'd accomplished the day we spent with the future teachers and slam poets. But they didn't want to focus on an event gone by. The end of the school year was approaching and they wanted a chance to share their work with another audience; they intuited the power inherent in this kind of action and they wanted to claim for themselves again the agency they'd enacted. Barbara suggested that we show the work to their families and friends in the community. So we invited them to the school to hear the children present some of their writing. We planned to begin at 5:00 and imagined a small number of guests from each class showing up; however, almost everyone (including parents, grandparents, siblings, cousins, and friends) invited by the children not only attended but they arrived early. They brought plentiful platters of food—salsa, tortillas, tamales, enchiladas, frijoles, and more. Some sat in large groups others, others in pairs, while they ate with family and friends and read their writing. I looked across the room and watched as Consuelo read her mom's story in English and then translated it into Spanish. Her mom kept pulling Consuelo closer; she had both arms around her when Consuelo reached the poem at the end (*The Giving One*, above) about her mom's determination to never give up. I looked over and smiled at Consuelo as she mouthed, "She's crying," nodding her head slightly towards her mom.

Counterportraiture and Hope for the Future

Part of our work involved rewriting the selves that the children had come to be and were forced into being in school; part of it required uncovering the truths in families and rural neighborhoods; and part of it focused on informing others in our own words of our truths. Poetry, which Bomer and Bomer (2001) described as the only medium that "has the grace to reside at funerals and weddings, to mark the transformations in peoples' lives, to say what cannot be said" (p. 3), underpinned our engagement in critical literacy. Our poetry and other writings were acts of "political resistance" (Espada, 1994) because these were about exposing false images in the official portrait by peeling off the thin layers of veneer in order to show the bold base colors beneath. Our counterportraits clarified the on-going struggle against the inaccurate picture of these children as literacy failures and the inappropriate and inequitable mandates to, therefore, delimit their school literacy curriculum.

Inspiring hope for children living at the nexus of multiple crises—economic, linguistic, familial, cultural, educational, to name a few—necessitates different kinds of curricular processes, like the ones we initiated by finding and naming the individual truths that children brought to school. The situation demanded changing the direction of our discussions about texts by others we had read and the ones we wrote ourselves from the personal to the critical (Lewis, 1999). Transformation was at the heart of the work because it facilitated our inquiry to know ourselves, others, and the world around us differently and much more clearly, as well as understand what makes it possible to influence others' thinking about all of this. We lived Lewison, Flint, & Van Sluys' (2002) "four dimensions [of critical literacy]: (1) disrupting the commonplace, (2) interrogating multiple viewpoints, (3) focusing on sociopolitical issues, and (4) taking action and promoting social justice" (p. 382).

In small but observable ways, the official portrait was challenged by our non-official portraits. Counterportraiture, then, is evidence of democratic process when democracy is considered as both an ideal and a political project. As an ideal, democracy can never be achieved because of the continuously changing nature of context. But as a political project, democracy is possible through collective efforts to share an ongoing struggle for understanding, clarification, interrogation, and enactment of this ever-emerging ideal. We repeatedly named, addressed, and renegotiated the demands that were placed upon us as children, family members, friends, community members, teachers and researchers. At the heart of that democratic process for us was naming our ongoing struggle (Shor and Freire, 1987; Valosinov, 1973), one that the children, their families, teachers and other advocates engaged in and experienced in their classrooms, school and community. We struggled to resist the demands of standards, standardized curriculum, and being standardized. We struggled to honor identities or, perhaps more accurately, subjectivities (Moje, 2002) that were specific to home, school, or community contexts, and to create spaces for writing truths, interrogating those truths, and presenting them to each other and others. We came to realize that the work of counterportraiture is never complete in a democracy because interrogating extant practices and policies needs to be an ongoing process, or we risk complying with the hegemonic realities that impose themselves on classrooms in which marginalized and disenfranchised children attend school. For those not working in classrooms, this work is equally important because conscientization—raising consciousnesses about issues of accuracy, decency, fairness, and justice—is the work of every student, teacher, classroom, school, family, and community, indeed every citizen, within a democratic society.

One noteworthy facet of this research was the struggle between the official demands placed upon the children, their teachers, and even their families and the non-official, but very real, demands that constitute their everyday lives. The official demands, situated in official policy mandates and implementation, call for standardized testing, AYP, prescriptive curriculum, and compliance. The non-official portraits, situated in the everyday, call for accuracy and clarity across different experiences and subjectivities, questioning what is taken for granted and disrupting practices and structures that marginalize or even ignore the specifics of local knowledge, language and culture. The hegemonic power of the official overshadows all literacy activity; the inquisitive nature of the unofficial is, so far, negligibly felt by the official. As we learned more about each other and the many contexts in which the children lived, thought, and wrote, we became clearer that better literacy does not cause better economic conditions. Instead, literacy accomplishments, especially those estimated by current mainstream measures, only improve when economic conditions improve (Street, 1995). Yet, those advocating for better test scores repeatedly overpower those advocating for the economically poor— especially those who are immigrant, brown, and bilingual.

Realizing that several serious issues are bracketed by an intense interest in performance on tests has, surprisingly, not discouraged me because I was witness to the children's processes and to teachers', future teachers', poets', and families' responses to the children's work. Counterportraiture is grassroots work and the work ahead may involve students and their families composing counterportraits that we work to bring to other public forums. Such work is the new demand that faces us; it is authenticity that addresses both the official and potential for non-official portraits.

As Greene (1995) reminds us, the time has come, once again, to hear from the silenced and the victimized, to challenge those whose actions perpetuate silencing and victimization, and to imagine ourselves into action:

> Again, it may be the recovery of imagination that lessens the social paralysis we see around us and restores the sense that something can be done in the name of what is decent and humane. (p. 34)

> We need . . . to recapture some of the experiences of coming together that occurred in the peace movement and the civil rights movement. We need to articulate what it signifies for some of us to support people with AIDS, to feed and house homeless persons in some dignified way, to offer day-long support to the very young in store-front schools, to bring into being teacher communities in our working spaces. (p. 197)

At the end of the school year, Barbara retired and moved to Texas to be closer to family; she eventually took a teaching job because she missed the classroom so much. She emails me occasionally and reflects upon the impact of the work on her practice. She constantly challenges team members in her current school, asking them why they persist to comply with practices that are so detrimental to the most needy students. Yet, she misses the support of our work together and does not know how long she will continue to teach. Patia was asked to teach bilingual second grade and is doing that at Mesa Vista. Honestly, the work did not influence her teaching of second grade. It was an intense year of research and she recalls it fondly, focusing most upon the relationships with Barbara and me. She misses our lunchtime discussions, but now works to comply with the requests of her second grade team and literacy leaders at the school. This neither surprises nor disappoints me; she's honest and believes the school makes the best decisions possible in terms of purchases of published programs for her students. Patia makes clear the need for sustained relationships in professional development and the way she teaches and makes decisions underscore the hegemonic nature of school and its powerful influence on teachers who lack a strong belief in teacher as decision maker. Patia makes clear the need for more work in collaborative ways.

Barbara and Patia's different responses to the work—and what they took from it—nag at the future of work in schools. Clearly, the work must be sustained for more than a year and beyond the tiny 'sample size' of two classrooms. Also, a single researcher is not able to reach the classrooms of an entire school, even if the entire staff desired to participate in the work. Therein lies another problem with future work. This work cannot be accomplished through traditional professional development means because those are typically instituted by administrators and decision makers in power, often and increasingly void of teacher input. The kind of work we did together was collective and demanded individuals invest time and energy with no known answers placed before them; these are ways of professional development that are contrary to what teachers have lived in most settings. These are professional development ways of thinking and being that are counter to the traditional portrait of professional development because we interrogated every aspect of our time together. Whereas many teachers work to comply, we worked to question. Whereas many teachers work to enact something that is already constructed, we worked to have the classroom as a site of construction (and struggle). Whereas many classrooms are places in which children cooperate (with a publisher's or legislative agenda), we worked to have the classroom as a place to inquire, demand, explain, and collectively create new knowledge.

Schools are not organized as places for teacher reflection and authentic and ongoing inquiry by teachers and their students. Parents are welcomed at many schools, particularly if they are willing to support the school's commitment to compliance to state and national trends. But these trends are hurting children at places like Mesa Vista and parents do not feel welcomed when they hear stories of their children's failures. They feel blamed. In spite of this, hope persists for me as a researcher, teacher, and new friend of some of the families in this study. I have hope because they do; moments such as Consuelo's in which parent and child feel affirmed in the results of a meaningful learning experience are the essence of hope. The current misguided trend towards standardizing children and curriculum will crumble because of moments such as these. The lies and lost dreams are named when they are written about and that naming shines a light on the depth of inequity and injustice—and that light is hope. And, finally, hope lies in collective work in which individuals matter and the good of all and for all is central.

I end with the words of Esperanza because she seems to have captured the goal of this work, a goal I had not previously articulated until the analysis of the year's worth of data. These young writers were previously unrecognized as writers because a repressive law, *No Child Left Behind*, constrained most possibilities for quality writing in the name of raising reading and math test scores. The children had, as Esperanza explains, minds that did not recognize their words, their power to name, explain, interrogate and disrupt and the possibility to challenge the world around them. Our year together gave them the opportunity to hear their voices do that work. Esperanza explained it this way:

I used to have a brain
Without words
But now
I do

References

Bomer, R. & Bomer, K. (2001). *For a better world: Reading and writing for social action.* Portsmouth: Heinemann.

Espada, M. (Ed.) (1994). *Poetry like bread: Poets of the political imagination.* Willimantic, CT: Curbstone Press.

Freire, P. (1970). The adult literacy process as cultural action for freedom. *Harvard Educational Review, 40* (2), 205-225.

Lewis, C. (1999). The Quality of the Question: Probing Culture in Literature-Discussion Groups. In C. Edelsky (Ed.). *Making justice our project: Teachers working toward critical whole language practice* (pp. 163-190). Urbana, Ill: National Council of Teachers of English.

Lewison, M., Flint, A.S., & Van Sluys, K. (2002). Taking on critical literacy: The journey of newcomers and novices. *Language Arts (79),* 5, 382-392. New York, New York: Palgrave.

Moje, E. (2002). Re-framing adolescent literacy research for new times: Studying youth as a resource. *Reading Research and Instruction, 41*(3), 211-227.

Shor, I. & Freire, P. (1987). *A pedagogy for liberation: Dialogues in transforming education.* Granby, MA: Bergin & Garvey.

Street, B. (1995). *Social literacies: Critical approaches to literacy in development, ethnography and education.* New York: Longman.

Volosinov, V.N. (1973). *Marxism and the philosophy of language* (L. Matejka & I.R. Titunik, Trans.). New York: Seminar Press. (Original work published in 1930).

SERIES THREE

READING THE (DE)COLONIZED WORLD: CULTURAL LITERACY FOR PUEBLO OF LAGUNA STUDENTS

CHAPTER EIGHT
LITERACY FROM A NATIVE VANTAGE POINT

Jeanette Haynes Writer
Lee Francis, IV
Gilbert Sanchez

Following Interstate 40, approximately 45 miles west of Albuquerque, New Mexico, lays K'awaika, the Pueblo of Laguna. Winding through red rock mesas, set within the pinion and juniper-filled desert landscape against the backdrop of Mt. Taylor, Laguna Pueblo spreads out into six villages: Mesita; Laguna; Paraje; Encinal; Paguate; and Seama. In their stories and within their collective consciousness, the spoken words of the Laguna People tell of living here in this homeland since time began. However, the history and science books of the outsiders assert and impose a written *truth* that the People's ancestors, like that of all Native Americans, were an earlier group of immigrants coming over the Bering Strait land bridge. They were simply an earlier group of immigrants roaming the landscape before European immigrants arrived and history began—bringing *civilized* knowledge and an *advanced* culture. Since the time of Europeans' entrance into the Pueblo landscape, a struggle has existed over right of place, right of being, and right to knowledge and voice.

In viewing Freire and Macedo's (1987) concept of *reading the world* we, as Indigenous People, two from Laguna Pueblo, and one from Cherokee Nation, discuss and problematize the struggle and pathway engaged by community members and educators within the Pueblo of Laguna to develop a curriculum for the Laguna History and Culture class offered at Laguna-Acoma High and Middle School from January 2003 to June 2005. This course served as a mechanism to speak back to the colonizer's history and construction of knowledge by centering the Laguna perspective, history, and knowledge. The class centered on Laguna Pueblo's culture, history, and a conceptualization of education for the community and its students.

Such a course is important for the Pueblo of Laguna on a number of levels, which we will explore in this chapter. As well, the course is important for other tribal communities, serving as a model in their endeavors to provide a culturally relevant and tribally-centered education for their children and youth.

Wrapped within the story we tell here is the critical exploration of the historical context of colonization, and interrogation and contestation of the present use of the terms *literacy* and *literate* within the No Child Left Behind (NCLB) Act and era. E. D. Hirsch, Jr. (1988) contends that for one to be considered *culturally literate* one must access the "network of information that all competent readers possess" (p. 2). This *network of information* or, rather, the official canon of knowledge belongs to the dominating society.[1] Further, Hirsch, Kett and Trefil (2002) assert, "No one in the English-speaking world can be considered literate without a basic knowledge of the Bible" (p. 1). Hirsch's concept of [reading] competency requires one to assimilate to the mainstream, and moves into the realm of standardization of both the person and her or his knowledge. This type of literacy leveraged within education policy and Westernized schooling structures operates as a means to continue the colonization of Indigenous Peoples. Utilizing the literature on colonization and the theoretical frameworks of Critical Race Theory and Tribal Critical Race Theory, we speak back to the continued colonizing efforts found within NCLB, name what we consider *literacy* and *literate* in the context of the Pueblo of Laguna, and discuss the development of critically literate and culturally literate Laguna Pueblo members through the Laguna History and Culture class.

It is important to state that while we came to the end of the George W. Bush administration's reign, under which NCLB was designed, implemented, and enforced, we see that NCLB has not been left behind by U.S. President Barack Obama, Education Secretary Arne Duncan, or other political representatives. As the Democratic presidential candidate, Barack Obama claimed NCLB reform by fully funding the law; providing *high quality* teachers to all students through recruitment, preparation, retention, and reward; and supporting schools in need of improvement rather than punishing them. At this time, however, we have yet to see significant changes to NCLB by President Obama or Secretary Duncan; following the NCLB agenda's heavy emphasis on standardized testing, the standardization of students through an assimilative curriculum continues. What we present here provides evidence that educationally imposed oppressions, the value of whiteness and white privilege, and practices of colonization have been the foundation of the educational terrain, and will most likely remain in U.S. schools even though NCLB may eventually be overhauled. Because of this history, and the associated contemporary conditions of ongoing assimilation and control, the development of tribally-centered curriculum is of utmost importance.

Colonization

To enter into a discussion of colonization, one must first have a working definition; we draw ours from Indigenous scholars Waziyatawin Angela Wilson and Michael Yellow Bird (2005):

> Colonization refers to both the formal and informal methods (behaviors, ideologies, institutions, policies, and economies) that maintain the subjugation or exploitation of Indigenous Peoples, lands, and resources. Colonizers engage in this process because it allows them to maintain and/or expand their social, political, and economic power. (p. 2)

European colonization of the Americas and of Indigenous Peoples is a historical fact: we will not spend time arguing this phenomenon within this chapter. Due to the history of colonization, and the ensuing all-encompassing Westernized system of institutions, Native Americans had, and in many ways, have, no part in the establishment or rules for public education. Westernized education policies— curriculum, pedagogy, etc.—have been imposed on Native Peoples for generations as enactments of colonization.

The Westernized system of education has served to disregard and suppress the sovereign status of Native Nations, and has halted or seriously constricted self-determination (Adams, 1995; Grande, 2004; Pewewardy, 2005, Szasz, 1999). Tribal sovereignty[2] may be defined as "the ability of a tribal community to control its own political, social, economic, and religious life," (Edmunds, 2012, p. 6), while self-determination can be defined as "the right of all peoples to freely determine their political status and freely pursue their economic, social, and cultural development" (Porter, 2005, p. 108).

Colonization is historically rooted and carries into our present reality through its overt and covert operations in various institutions and systems. Wilson and Yellow Bird (2005) emphasize that, "[t]he current institutions and systems are designed to maintain the privilege of the colonizer and the subjugation of the colonized, and to produce generations of people who will never question their position within this relationship" (p. 1). Ashcroft, Griffiths and Tiffin (1995) remind us that the imperial process, thus colonization, "works *through* as well as *upon* individuals and societies" (p. 3). As such, we examine colonization and the effects of its legacy that occurs through teachers, administrators, and schools, purposefully or not, consciously or not, upon Students of Color and, in our instance, upon Laguna Pueblo students. We interrogate colonization through the tools provided by Critical Race Theory and Tribal Critical Race Theory.

Critical Race Theory and Tribal Critical Race Theory

Critical Race Theory (CRT) developed out of the field of critical legal studies and works to examine entrenched, but often subtle, racism. One assumption of CRT is that we live in a racist society and that racism is protected through laws, social beliefs and actions, as well as through the media and the master narrative,[3] or, using Gee's (2001) scholarship on literacy, through dominating societal discourses. Critical race theorists study the relationship between race, racism and power, and add an activist dimension, thus, transforming that relationship (Delgado & Stefancic, 2001).

The primary goal and benefit of CRT is the construction of an alternative reality by way of naming one's reality through storytelling: "Social reality is constructed by the formulation and the exchange of stories about individual situations" (Ladson-Billings & Tate, 1995, p. 57). This storytelling allows writers and thinkers to "analyze the myths, presuppositions, and received wisdoms that make up the common culture about race and that invariably render...minorities one-down" (Delgado, 1995, p. xiv). For researchers, CRT offers a tool which provides "greater ontological and epistemological understanding of how race and racism affect the education and lives of the racially disenfranchised" (Parker & Lynn, 2002, pp. 7-8). Ladson-Billings and Tate (1995) transitioned CRT from the field of law to the field of education, followed by others who identified the permanent nature of racism within educational institutions and structures and utilized the valuable aspect of counterstorytelling as valid knowledge. Counterstories "challenge, displace or mock...pernicious [master] narratives" (Delgado & Stefancic, 2001, p. 43) and serve to combat the marginalization and silencing of the lived experiences of Students of Color in dominant educational discourse (Solórzano & Yosso, 2001).

Indigenous scholars (Haynes Writer, 2002; Hermes, 1999; Rains, 2003; Williams, 1995, 1997) began employing CRT to examine the effects of race, racism, and power on Native Nations and in Native communities, utilizing it as a mechanism to perform truth-telling—to speak back to colonization and oppression. For the Indigenous community, CRT offers a means in which to present and critique colonization in a broader perspective, a more inclusive perspective. Brayboy (2005) used as his foundation CRT to introduce Tribal Critical Race Theory (TribalCrit).[4] TribalCrit examines issues of Indigenous Peoples in relationship to the United States and its laws and policies. Although a significant role is played by racism, a primary tenet within TribalCrit is the endemic nature of colonization and its processes in society. We use TribalCrit here to interrogate the colonization in Laguna Pueblo, in the educational context and experience of Laguna students, and examine its presence in educational directives influenced by NCLB and its narrow conceptualization of literacy. We utilize CRT and TribalCrit to present an alternative reality, a Laguna Pueblo reality, to formulate and transform education, literacy, and what it means to be a culturally literate Laguna Pueblo member. In this essay we draw upon both CRT and TribalCrit to construct the *story* of NCLB by speaking back to colonization through the development and teaching of the Laguna History and Culture class. We assert that in order to speak of and about Indigenous experiences, one has to speak to and through the historical condition of colonization—it is a requisite in utilizing CRT. Thus, utilizing TribalCrit, colonization and its resistance are inherent threads woven within the stories that Indigenous Peoples tell.

The Emergence of this Story and its Methodology

Our story here is told by Lee Francis, IV, who taught the Laguna History and Culture class; Gilbert Sanchez, who served as Superintendent of the Pueblo of Laguna

Department of Education (LDoE) for 15 years; and Jeanette Haynes Writer, Associate Professor at New Mexico State University (NMSU). Lee's ancestry is from Laguna Pueblo; Gilbert is from both Laguna and Jemez Pueblos; and Jeanette is Tsalagi (a citizen of Cherokee Nation). The telling of this story transpired over 20 years, emerging through multiple forms.

In 1990, Jeanette moved from Oklahoma to Grants, New Mexico, and worked as the academic counselor at the NMSU-Grants campus; she worked there for two years before leaving to pursue her doctorate. The NMSU-Grants campus is located approximately 35 miles from Laguna Pueblo. It was at this time that she became familiar with individuals from the Pueblo of Laguna, as well as aware of their history and the tensions that existed in the larger Grants community and school system, specifically for Laguna-Acoma High School. Through enduring personal friendships over the years with Laguna community members and her presence in the community for activities such as Feast Days, occasional ceremonial activities, and family events, Jeanette came to know more intimately the history and culture of the Laguna People and their individual and collective struggles and successes of self-determining educational initiatives.

Jeanette became a NMSU faculty member in 1996 in the Department of Curriculum and Instruction in Las Cruces. She moved back to Grants in 2005 to oversee her department's extension of its master's degree program at the NMSU-Grants campus and to assist with the Elementary Education teacher education program at the campus. During that time the Pueblo of Laguna was in the midst of carrying out community activities with support from a Kellogg Leadership for Community Change (KLCC) grant.[5] Jeanette's long-time friend and Pueblo of Laguna Board of Education member, Dr. Shelly Valdez, served as a facilitator of the grant. She initiated the meeting of Gilbert and Jeanette. Although Gilbert and Jeanette had met in the 1990s when they were both involved in work with the Commission on the Future of Laguna Education, it was not until he invited her to participate with the KLCC group in January 2006, that Gilbert and Jeanette began discussions regarding Indigenous education. It was also through the KLCC activities that Lee and Jeanette met. Jeanette welcomed the opportunity work in the community and to participate with Pueblo of Laguna's education initiatives.

Because of her work in teacher education and Indigenous education, Gilbert asked Jeanette to serve as chair for the KLCC Curriculum Committee; the charge of the committee was the development of a philosophy statement to guide the vision of education in the Eastern Cibola County Schools Consortium (ECCSC). Gilbert and Jeanette shared personal and professional philosophies that education could and should be culturally and community-centered and often discussed the challenge of NCLB Act directives on Native cultural continuance and Native-centered curriculum.

Gilbert and Jeanette's work through KLCC developed into a partnership between NMSU and the Pueblo of Laguna Department of Education. This partnership led to the acquisition of a teacher quality grant to recruit and retain individuals from the ECCSC area who had an associate's degree, assisting and supporting them in obtaining their bachelor's degrees in early childhood education or elementary education. This partnership promoted the KLCC's plans, goals, and objectives by developing classroom and community leaders and supported the educational process in the Pueblo to encourage and maintain cultural continuance and tribal sovereignty.

Wilson and Yellow Bird's (2005) *For Indigenous Eyes Only: A Decolonization Handbook* was published at the time that Gilbert asked Jeanette to participate with KLCC. This text was designed as a workbook that individuals and communities could utilize to facilitate discussions on the conditions of Native Peoples and communities. Gilbert and Jeanette had a copy of this book and discussed the writers' concepts and perspectives on colonization, conversing on the embedded-ness of colonization within the Westernized education system and the possibilities Native communities had to decolonize the curriculum and schooling processes for their children and youth.

The project of weaving the story surrounding the Laguna History and Culture class was born, emerging out of Jeanette and Gilbert's dialogues regarding colonization, decolonization, self-determination and sovereignty. Concepts and ideas from the *For Indigenous Eyes Only* text helped to situate the conversations between Lee, Gilbert, and Jeanette—especially as they discussed NCLB's effect on Native communities. It was apparent that the NCLB Act legislated and privileged standardized curricula situated within *whitestream*[6] (Denis, 1997) culture and knowledge structures, mandating high stakes testing which reinforced the standardized curricula and pedagogy, and positioned literacy as only the reading of the printed word. NCLB further alienated Native communities from the schooling enterprise by barring Native language and culture from the curriculum in lieu of a whitestreamed curriculum to meet NCLB mandates (Beaulieu, 2008) regardless of research that validated Native culturally-based education (Demmert & Towner, 2003). Educational directives imposed from the outside, through federal and state mandates driving the *accountability, adequate yearly progress* (AYP), *high quality,* and *high achievement* discourse, did not consider cultural imperatives or Indigenous ways of knowing— tribal cultural literacy—within the Pueblo community and its schools. Discussions of colonization and decolonization within the *For Indigenous Eyes Only* text supported tribal self-determination and sovereignty actions that Gilbert, Jeanette, and others were striving for, even if they were not named as such, in the educational context for Native students they worked with.

To create our story here, Jeanette held conversational interviews with Gilbert and Lee: one interview with each of them individually, and one interview with them together. Other informal conversations occurred between Gilbert, Lee, and Jeanette which also situated this story. To weave this story together, Jeanette returned to a method that she and her colleague, Rudolfo Chávez Chávez, utilized in previous work as critical multicultural teacher educators.[7] Through dialogue between Lee, Gilbert, and Jeanette, a story was created—or woven—to tell of the creation and process of the Laguna History and Culture class and the importance of such a course for the cultural literacy of Pueblo of Laguna youth. Utilizing CRT and TribalCrit, the master narrative supporting and legislating whitestreaming within NCLB was challenged with a counterstory privileging Laguna perspectives, history, and knowledge.

As well, a survey of historical and education texts and documents provided additional resources, such as LDoE documents; Pueblo of Laguna member Nick Cheromiah's (2004) *Laguna History* text; KLCC documents; newspaper articles; and Internet sources. Jeanette's interactions through the years with Pueblo of Laguna college/university-level students and community members[8] and dialogue with various Pueblo educators and school personnel provided further insight and form for this transformative story so others may read our collective words to become more literate as they *read the [Laguna] world* and educational context.

Within the framework of CRT, stories are created and told utilizing various structures: analysis of musical lyrics, historical documents, narratives, parables, and poetry (Delgado, 1995; Olivas, 1995; Ross, 1995). In this essay, we construct a question-and-answer dialogue between Lee, Gilbert, and Jeanette to state the reasons for the development of the Laguna History and Culture class and to "identify, analyze, and transform subtle and overt forms of racism in education in order to transform society" (Solórzano & Yosso, 2001, pp. 31-32). The dialogue is interspersed with education research literature and Native American and Laguna history; brackets are utilized where that occurs to inform the reader beyond the words of the dialogue.

References

Adams, D. W. (1995). *Education for extinction: American Indians and the boarding school experience, 1875-1928.* Lawrence, KS: University Press of Kansas.

Ashcroft, B., Griffiths, G., & Tiffin, H. (Eds.). (1995). *The post-colonial studies reader.* New York: Rutledge.

Beaulieu, D. (2008). Native American research and policy development in an era of No Child Left Behind: Native language and culture during the administrations of Presidents Clinton and Bush. *Journal of American Indian Education, 47*(1), 10-45.

Brayboy, B. M. J. (2005, December).Toward a tribal critical race theory in education. *The Urban Review, 37*(5), 425-446.

Cheromiah, N. (2004). *Laguna History: First edition.* Laguna, NM: private printing.

Delgado, R. (Ed.). (1995). *Critical race theory: The cutting edge.* Philadelphia: Temple University Press.

Delgado, R., & Stefancic, J. (2001). *Critical race theory: An introduction.* New York: NYU Press.

Demmert, W. G., & Towner, J. C. (2003). *A review of the research literature on the influences of culturally based education on the academic performance of Native American students.* Portland, OR: Northwest Regional Educational Laboratory.

Denis, C. (1997). *We are not you: First Nations and Canadian modernity.* Toronto: Broadview.

Edmunds, R. D. (2012). Introduction: Twentieth-century warriors. In R. D. (Ed.), *The new warriors: Native American leaders since 1900* (pp. 1-15). Lincoln, NE: University of Nebraska Press.

Freire, P., & Macedo, D. (1987). *Literacy: Reading the word and the world.* New York: Bergin & Garvey.

Gee, J. P. (2001). What is literacy? In P. Shannon (Ed.), *Becoming political, too: New readings and writings on the politics of literacy education* (pp. 1-9). New Hampshire: Heinemann.

Grande, S. (2004). Red pedagogy: Native American social and political thought. Lanham, MD: Rowman & Littlefield.

Haynes Writer, J. (2002). Terrorism in Native America: Interrogating the past, examining the present, and constructing a liberatory future. *Anthropology & Education Quarterly, 33*(3), 317330.
Hermes, M. (1999). Research methods as a situated response: Toward a First Nations' methodology. In L. Parker, D. Deyhle, & S. Villenas (Eds.), *Race is...race isn't: Critical race theory and qualitative studies in education* (pp. 83-100). Boulder, CO: Westview Press.
Hirsch, E. D., Jr. (1988). *Cultural literacy: What every American needs to know.* New York: Vintage Books.
Hirsch, E. D., Jr., Kett, J. F., & Trefil, J. (2002). *The new dictionary of cultural literacy: What every American needs to know.* New York: Houghton Mifflin.
Ladson-Billings, G., & Tate, W. (1995). Toward a critical race theory of education. *Teachers College Record, 97*(1), 47-68.
No Child Left Behind Act of 2001, Pub. L. No. 107-110, § 101 *et seq.* (2001).
Olivas, M. A.(1995). The chronicles, my grandfather's stories, and immigration law: The slave traders chronicle as racial history. In R. Delgado (Ed.), *Critical race theory: The cutting edge* (pp. 9-20). Philadelphia, PA: Temple University Press.
Parker, L., & Lynn, M. (2002). What's race got to do with it? Critical race theory's conflicts with and connections to qualitative research and epistemology. *Qualitative Inquiry, 8*(1), 7-22.
Pewewardy, C. (2005). Ideology, power, and the miseducation of Indigenous Peoples in the United States. In W. A. Wilson & M. Yellow Bird (Eds.), *For Indigenous eyes only: A decolonization handbook* (pp. 139-156). Santa Fe, NM: School of America Research Press.
Porter, R. O. (2005). The decolonization of Indigenous governance. In W. A. Wilson & M. Yellow Bird (Eds.), *For Indigenous eyes only: A decolonization handbook* (pp. 87-108). Santa Fe, NM: School of America Research Press.
Rains, F. V. (2003). To greet the dawn with open eyes: American Indians, white privilege and the power of residual guilt in the social studies. In G. Ladson-Billings (Ed.), *Critical race theory perspectives on the social studies: The profession, policies, and curriculum* (pp. 199-227). Greenwich, CT: Information Age Publishing.
Ross, T. (1995). The Richmond narratives. In R. Delgado (Ed.), *Critical race theory: the cutting edge* (pp. 38-47). Philadelphia, PA: Temple University Press.
Solórzano, D. G., & Yosso, T. J. (2001). From racial stereotyping and deficit discourse toward a critical race theory in teacher education. *Multicultural Education, 9*(1), 2-8.
Szasz, M. C. (1999). *Education and the American Indian: The road to self-determination since 1928.* Albuquerque, NM: University of New Mexico Press.
Williams, R. A., Jr. (1995). Documents of barbarism: The contemporary legacy of European racism and colonialism in the narrative traditions of federal Indian law. In R. Delgado (Ed.)*Critical Race Theory: The cutting edge,* pp. 98-109. Philadelphia, PA: Temple University Press.
Williams, R. A., Jr. (1997). Vampires anonymous and critical race practice. *Michigan Law Review*, 95, 741–765.
Wilson, A. W., & Yellow Bird, M. (Eds.). (2005). *For Indigenous eyes only: A decolonization handbook.* Santa Fe, NM: School of America Research Press.

Notes

[1] Weight is given here to the term *dominating* instead of *dominant* to emphasize that colonization and its processes are a continuous reality for Indigenous Peoples.

[2] Although we have provided a definition for sovereignty here, it must be stated that no single definition has been accepted by Indigenous Peoples. For more insight to the de-

bate over the definitions and parameters of sovereignty, see Robert Warrior's (2008) article, "Organizing American Indian and Indigenous Studies."

³ The master narrative, also referred to as the grand narrative or metanarrative, encompasses the large-scale or grand theories, philosophies, or stories about the world and acts as the only explanation for knowledge or historical experience. See Jean-Francois Lyotard (1984) in *The Postmodern-Condition: A Report on Knowledge*.

⁴ CRT has been embraced by a number of groups which have sculpted CRT to be useful to their specific historicized, racialized, or gendered conditions, such as LatCrits, FemCrits and AsianCrits.

⁵ The Pueblo of Laguna Department of Education (LDoE) applied for and received a grant of $279,000 in 2002 from the New Mexico Community Foundation through an initiative called the Kellogg Leadership for Community Change Grant funded by the W.K. Kellogg Foundation. With LDoE serving as the host organization, the KLCC Grant and subsequent activities supported the continued collaboration between the distinct cultural communities in the neighboring communities, including the Spanish Land Grants, to improve educational planning and programs for the students served within the schools in Eastern Cibola County. A sub-committee of the KLCC was the Curriculum Committee of which Gilbert asked Jeanette to chair in 2006.

⁶ Denis discusses "whitestream" in terms of society being more than demographically white, society is primarily built on the white experience, and thus, its institutions are developed and operate from that frame of reference.

⁷ See Haynes Writer & Chávez Chávez (2001), "Storied Lives, Dialog→Retro-Reflections: Melding Critical Multicultural Education and Critical Race Theory for Pedagogical Transformation." Jeanette is grateful to Rudolfo Chávez Chávez for introducing her to CRT and for his mentorship and continued friendship as a faculty colleague.

⁸ See Haynes Writer & Oesterreich (2011) for a detailed account of the obstacles and successes experienced by a cohort of Pueblo women who were working toward their bachelor's degrees to become degreed teachers.

CHAPTER NINE
THE LAGUNA HISTORY AND CULTURE CLASS

Jeanette Haynes Writer
Lee Francis, IV
Gilbert Sanchez

The introduction of the Laguna Pueblo people to non-Natives, specifically, Europeans, came in the form of the invasion of the Spanish Conquistadors in the 1500s. When the Spaniards arrived, they found the People living in established settlements, or villages, utilizing sophisticated agricultural techniques in the farmlands within the arid landscape and governing themselves in a complex leadership system that had been in place for generations. Yet, the Laguna People were proclaimed as and written to be *primitive*. Years of enduring genocide, rape, slavery, and widespread exploitation of the Pueblo Peoples by the Spaniards resulted in the Pueblo Rebellion of 1680, which gave the Pueblo Peoples respite from Spanish domination; however, the relief was short lived.

Although it had long existed before the arrival of the Europeans and their historical record, the Pueblo of Laguna was established in 1699 when the People living at K'awaika were proclaimed by the Governor of New Mexico to be of the renamed community of San José de la Laguna, shortened to Laguna a short time later (Cheromiah, 2004). This *beginning with the Europeans* history comprises the master narrative advanced in the public schools and dominating societal discourse—the Laguna History and Culture class and this counterstory serves to write/right the story.

Jeanette: Gilbert, I'll start with you. You've served as the Superintendent of the Pueblo of Laguna Department of Education for more than 14 years. How did the idea for the Laguna History and Culture class emerge?

Gilbert: Having the experience of working at Laguna since 1985 as an assistant principal, principal, and then superintendent, and looking at our students' offerings, it was always in the back of my mind that we needed to develop a history course for our youth.

We made an attempt of teaching about the Jackpile Uranium Mine[1] when the staff wrote a grant and obtained funds to develop the curriculum for the Jackpile Mine. Another curriculum component was the law-and-order piece where the students learned about jurisdictional issues, learning where the state, county, and local police have jurisdiction. That developed as the result of questions into the curriculum, addressing it based on our needs. My thinking was: Why can't we do this for the whole cultural piece? But we didn't have the resources or the time or the staff to really address that.

I began talking to a friend of mine who has since passed on, Lee Francis, III, Lee's father. Lee's father was a professor at the University of New Mexico and I shared my ideas with him about the class as I was working on it: identifying topics like education, tribal government, community, the Jackpile Mine, the law-and-order code, and economic development. I had the idea to use community members for the presentations and present the research that's available. I thought of it as a class to take place after school or something along those lines. In a meeting I had with Lee, III, he said, "I found somebody to teach the course." I said, "Oh, who is this person?" He replied, "It's my son, Lee. I want him to come home. I think he could do this piece, and I'll help him with it." And that's how the whole program got started.

I had also been talking to the Grants/Cibola School District to get funds for the course through the Indian education funding that they receive. I showed them an outline and some of the things we were going to do. Luckily they didn't ask for a whole curriculum piece from me; what they were really concerned with was who the person teaching the course was going to be. Lee didn't have a degree in teaching; he had a bachelor's degree in theatre. But under the guidance of one of the licensed school staff he was able to teach the course. We didn't have a lot of material, but we had a lot of ideas and we were able to sell them on that.

Lee: At the time I was working with the Bureau of Indian Affairs in Washington, DC. I just wanted a change because I had been traveling a lot—I wanted to get home. From the time I arrived I had about a month turnaround to learn as much as I possibly could. The initial framework was what Gilbert and my father put together along with some other community members in the initial planning phase. We put our heads together and came up with critical elements that we believed were important to the Laguna culture.

Jeanette: How long did you teach this course?

Lee: I taught the course from January 2003 until the end of June 2005. It ended up being three academic years total because we had a half year, spring 2003, where we compressed the class into one semester. We had the whole 2003-2004 school year and then 2004-2005.

The Past into the Present: What Youth Need to Know

Jeanette: Gilbert, from a Laguna cultural perspective, what do young people need to know to be culturally literate Laguna Pueblo members? What are some basic ideas, concepts, or philosophies?

Gilbert: I think a basic idea involves the historical piece, as well as the development of Laguna; that is, the development of our tribal government and community development.

Jeanette: Lee, picking up on the question from your perspective, what are those things that the young people need to know about their community or their people?

Lee: What I always started off with, and it was the hardest thing for me to get through to the kids, was the fact that the culture is not dead. That Laguna culture is not something in the past, it continues. And that was what I tried to stress throughout the year, to know that it's not boxed up. They learned of the changes that took place and how we've adapted to survive and thrive.

One of the things that I remember telling them in the beginning was, "You're going to get out of this [Laguna] world, and travel beyond these [school] doors. When you get to college or into the workforce, you're just an Indian; and even to other Indians, you're just an Indian." Initially, for the most part, I wouldn't get a response. And so I would continue, "What sets you apart is you know your history." One can talk to other Nations, to other tribal people, and they know their history, even if it's the pop culture part of it. What's ours? What was the Pueblo Revolt?[2] What is different about our system than any other system in the United States is the fact that we were brought in under a land grant and that we weren't made a reservation until 1918. We were honored as sovereign nations, all the Pueblos were. After the Pueblo Revolt, Laguna became the *cosmopolitan* Pueblo, because all these other people that were coming in had all these traditions. We have Acoma traditions; we have Navajo clans and traditions from the Long Walk;[3] and we have Isleta traditions from when the traditionalists were coming back up and from the intermarrying down there. So you have Santo Domingo, you have Jemez; you have all these people that came in, and all these groups that make up Laguna. I think that that's critically important for our youth to know. When they get out into the world that's how they're able to function and say, "I know my history." That falls under self-determination, individual self-determination; that individual sovereignty of "I know who I am, and you can't mess with that."

I wanted the students to learn about education—the old ways of learning and how it has evolved. So it does come back to that idea that the culture didn't die, that it just continues to evolve. And that it's *their* job to make sure it continues to thrive and evolve, and that one of those first steps is to know the history.

Oral History and Storytelling—Then and Now

Native intellectual and historian Donald L. Fixico (2003) delineates between oral history, "an event told orally" (p. 22), and oral tradition, which is a process within tribal communities. Oral tradition is complex, and functions as the "socio-cultural history of the community" (p. 23), defining what is important to that community. Oral history, thus individual stories, is literature told orally, and part of the process of the oral tradition. Each story, according to Fixico, is "an entity of power" (p. 22). It is through the stories of tribal communities that traditional knowledge is shared with subsequent generations; therefore, ensuring the continuance of that tribal community. At the 2002 National Indian Education Association Convention, Dr. Manu Aluli Meyer, a Hawaiian Native, stated in her keynote address that educators must consider the oral tradition and stories as part of what is meant by being *literate* (Meyer, 2002).

Jeanette: Can you talk to me about oral history, oral stories, and their place here?

Gilbert: The oral history and stories are central to sustainability of our way of life, religion and culture. It still is the main process that supports tribal members as they prepare for ceremonies, decision-making by our village officials, and is central to many other tribal and family matters. The loss of language is a critical issue and the culture is being affected by it, as a result it becomes important to document many of the stories that our elders tell. Documenting them will help our youth and future generations understand and maintain our cultural perspective.

Lee: In teaching the students, I wanted them to know about the old way we did storytelling and the way that we do it now. I wanted them to know about, of course, the history that came out of the oral stories. I could always see presence of the oral storytelling in the writing and could always tell in the writing that they were Laguna kids; they kind of rambled on like they were telling a story. But I wanted to teach them various forms of communication so I did an additive approach to developing their skills.[4] I would tell them, "I know this is the way you talk, and that's okay when we're having conversations. Sometimes I'm going to let it slide but you have to learn to use a period! [laughs] And you've got to learn to how to end this thing with something other than "And that's all I have to say."

I remember very specifically the conversation I had with my dad: he said, "Laguna stories never end they just kind of stop." There's not like "And that's just the way it was." He said they just stop. They stop being a story at that point in terms of us saying it out loud. He said, "You see that with all kids. It's just the way we are in general." But it's the reason why Laguna stories don't end. It's fascinating to see that they write the exact same way. They just get to a point and they say, "Alright, I'm just going to stop talking now," and that's the end of the paper.

Perspectives on Learning, Literacy and Achievement

Jeanette: I would like to move into talking about learning being equated with strictly *achievement* and the performance of Laguna students as successful students in both the context of Westernized schooling and their community. Gilbert, can you speak to that issue from what you've observed?

Gilbert: Yes. Years ago when I was a teacher I began looking at the educational growth of the students. I noticed a big disparity between the Indian kids and non-Indian kids, in terms of how successful they were in school. I wanted to know more about why some kids weren't as successful academically when they were successful everywhere else. To this day I'm still spurred on by that interest of *why*.

For me, this whole idea of student achievement is still there. And it has been quite a challenge to try to put it in perspective with people I am working with; not only colleagues, but other schools or systems. Achievement means different things to different people. I've been in education for over 35 years and I always remember looking at the first comparison of how well kids did in class—Indian kids were some of the lowest academically performing students and that's still the same today. I'm still thinking: Why? Why is that? That's one of the more difficult questions. We all know there are a lot of reasons why, but now I'm getting frustrated myself with how slow things have been to change, to really get to the part about where we talk about learning and translate learning into students being successful at school.

Jeanette: I agree. There are many reasons why but only a few are investigated. Living within this NCLB era, achievement is only considered in terms of standardized test scores. We're operating strictly out of the paradigm of Whiteness, but not naming it within the NCLB Act, and students' backgrounds and cultures are not spoken of except to name them in terms of who needs intervention.[5] So public schooling is operating out of the deficit theory or deficit thinking model which presumes that a student's failure in school is due to her or his *inherent* deficiencies, usually based on the student's and their family's cultural, economic, language, etc., identities, any of those that are not valued or considered the norm within the dominating society.[6] Essentially, Native students' achievement and literacy is focused on in terms of what they do not have, rather than what they bring to school—this deficit theory perspective has plagued Indigenous students since their entrance into Westernized schooling.[7]

With NCLB I specifically observe an extreme focus on the reading of the printed word, writing for the dominating society's type of assignments to express knowledge in a limited way, and having students swallow information and regurgitate it for the test. Lee, in having your own history from this community, and in what you were doing in the class, how do you view NCLB's impact on the students here at Laguna?

Lee: While working on my master's degree in educational leadership, in class we had debates on NCLB. What a great idea: You don't want to leave a child behind. But the problem comes into the execution of how you're trying to do that. I do think the Westernized method of assessing students' learning very much comes into conflict with us because it's not our way. It plays into a lot of the problems that have been identified over and over again in studies and testimonies that minority kids, especially Indian kids, don't take tests very well so we need more authentic and culturally relevant assessments.[8] But the kids are verbal and they can answer all the questions—they know the answers to them. Give them a little extra time and they can figure it out. A lot of the time the students don't see the necessity for some of the curriculum or classes, they say "I'm living at home. Why do I need to know algebra?" So I think it does come into conflict.

It is definitely the deficit theory model. We don't say, "Wow, this is amazing that you got six out of ten right, how awesome is that!" Instead, it's "You got four wrong." It doesn't take into consideration the visual learners. You have it with math, but it's still a lot of reading. You have reading and essay tests. In present form, the education under NCLB doesn't engage the students. From my research into this issue, I'm seeing it across the country. I think that Native students, in particular, and all students, in general, are less and less seeing the delivery of an education of engagement. It's not for us; it's not organic. It's concrete; it's an industrial system.

Jeanette: There is a big difference between a standardized curriculum and a curriculum with standards. You know, do we want to standardize our children?

Lee: Exactly. Trying to fit kids into this idea of educational standardization is problematic: "Well my kid's not learning as much as this kid over here, so therefore he's not prepared." I think that in one sense it's good if we're looking at learning potential, but in another sense it's bad because not all kids are going to learn the same. They are all going to be interested in something that is different from their peers. If you have a flexible enough curriculum that you can adapt, and say, "You know what, you're an awesome artist. Let's work on that; let's foster that. Let's get you a portfolio." I'm thinking how they can succeed. I think that is what NCLB limits. That's the problem. It especially doesn't work out on the rez because the kids don't want to be standardized.

Creativity in teaching: I think that's what's *lost*. You can get yourself into a bind with benchmarks, and standards, and the curriculum that you have to follow because you have to pass the test. I don't want the kids to pass the test, I want them to think! Being literate is being able to think.

Curriculum Content and Process

Jeanette: Lee, in terms of curriculum for the course, did that come from what your dad and Gilbert had set up? And, then, you added to it and built on it?

Lee: They had laid out the structure of all these particular areas that they wanted to cover: history, education, economics, and government. And then all the other elements that add to a culture, like food, art, music, and all those other things that weave their way throughout what culture means. Initially it was set up to have speakers from the community come in everyday, but it's really hard to get speakers to do that. So, out of necessity, over a couple of the summers, Gilbert and I worked on building the actual curriculum so as to meet the benchmarks and standards, assignments, lesson plans, and all the rest of that. Over the three years that we taught it, we worked on refining it to address the finer points of it by adding sections here and there. Mostly we were looking to try and create a total narrative of what culture included (i.e. music, art, language, religion, education, history, etc., and how all those parts were included in Laguna culture). For example, food was something we split off on its own. Originally the language was going to be woven in, and it was, but then I decided to make it a separate section all together so that the kids would have one section specifically addressing language. Then we added games and projects and writing assignments and reflective pieces and biographies and community interviews and interactions. We kept expanding what we could pass on to the students. It was a big change from just having a guest speaker and a summary essay. I did fine tuning over time, and then saw what the students responded to in their assignments.

Appropriate Knowledge and the Right to Know in the School Context

According to the 1879 Third Annual Report of the Laguna Mission, the crime of not attending Christian services was a violation of Catholic Church *law* at Laguna Pueblo, drawing harsh punishment from the Spanish:

> These [church] buildings were filled on Sundays and Holidays with Indians, not because they were willing, but because they were compelled to attend. Many of the Laguna people remember when the whipping of their people was a common thing. The Priests made the town Officers bring those who would not attend Mass to the Church door on the Sabbath morning and publicly whip them till he said it was enough. (Cheromiah, 2004, pp. 21-22).... For the most part, the native religion became covert, but it still flourished. Traditional religious activities happened at night and in secret. The most sacred dances took place away from the village. Non-Indian people were not allowed to participate in or observe the ceremonies, so the participants and artifacts could be kept safe from abuse and destruction like what had previously occurred. (Cheromiah, 2004, p. 20)

Jeanette: In Westernized education, curriculum is expected to be formally written out in lessons and objectives, knowledge or information about the various subjects is to be presented as planned and objective. But in this community, and this specific educational context, the presentation of and appropriateness of some information was conditional, correct?

Gilbert: We've always been cautioned by the traditionalists or the elders about how much we share. Our culture is an oral culture, relating the stories, oral storytelling, through word of mouth. Of course the religion goes with that; and the language goes the same way, too. That caution is clearly emphasized.[9] So when you first come in as a non-Indian, it can be confusing in regard to what people say. They'll tell you, you can't say this, you can't share that. So it can make it difficult for what's real and what can be shared.

Now when we get to the religious part, that's a whole other thing I always try to separate. With the class we didn't get into that piece but of course how do you not get into it, just naturally speaking. Along the way we kind of know what that is, as tribal members, or how much we share. We know enough that if we start going down that road we kind of know where to draw the line. So with that, it becomes a family responsibility, from that ceremonial, religious-type of activity that takes place.

Lee: Yes, in the class the only thing that we really didn't cover, that's off limits, is any of the religious content. That's pretty forbidden with us, just in general—you don't talk about that. That was the kind of thing we tiptoed around. But because I had a lot of the kids that had done ceremonial activities, they knew what I was saying when I would get into those particular areas, like "We're not going any farther than that, but we're going to address particular aspects." And if one of the community members or an elder came in and decided to talk about certain aspects of it, then that was all right. I had older folks come in and talk to the kids, and explain some things, but not into detail, obviously. But, there were some particular aspects that they would talk about, and then we were able to talk about it in class.

Jeanette: When I taught the undergraduate Multicultural Education (MCE) course here at Laguna Pueblo, I sensed the careful way of addressing those beliefs in public discourse. Because I have known people from the community for a long time, and have been invited to some activities, I have some insight to the religious beliefs and practices at the Pueblo, but I have been helped, permitted, if you will, to develop cultural literacy regarding the community. The students in the course would bring into the discussions issues around the religion and how it was or was not brought into or allowed into the school setting and in their classrooms. We could talk in class about some things very broadly; however, it was also very clear what was enough, and where we would not be going. I'm a Native person, but I'm not from this community and I do not have the right to know anything. So, it was the students who taught me, choosing what stories would be told, asking the questions, and deciding where we would or would not go.

I've thought about this pedagogically, and it was a very different MCE course than when teaching in Las Cruces in a number of ways. One, it was a class composed of all Native students, all Laguna women, and myself as a Native professor. This in itself brought us to explore and interrogate education and issues of power very differently than any other MCE course I've taught since I began teaching the course in 1996. We critiqued various issues and ideas from a Native perspective. The Native worldview was not merely privileged in this course. It was the course. Had this course been instructed by a non-Native professor, it would have been vastly different. Secondly, I shifted, both consciously and unconsciously, my pedagogical strategies. When entering into discourse which dealt with religious content, I pulled back from asking the inquiry-based questions—those questions used to probe issues deeper. Whereas, within the critical MCE framework, I'm the course facilitator and guide our journey of inquiry; here I changed this as well. The students decided where and how we would go. In the Westernized world, at the center of the quantitative and qualitative research paradigms is the assumption of the *right to know*.[10] As an Indigenous person I strongly oppose that notion. Some knowledge is not to be known by everyone; and there are processes and protocols to bring people into certain knowledge and to judge when someone is ready for particular knowledge. It is ultimately the property of the People.[11]

Gilbert: Yes, as a result of the colonization by the Spaniards and later the Americans and the assimilation policies, Pueblo People have essentially made any explanation, sharing of information, and some cultural/religious activities off limits to non-Indians, and in some cases off limits to even Indian people not of their tribe. Children are taught at the earliest ages not to share information about their culture and religious beliefs. It becomes inherent in tribal communities to respect other tribes' values and beliefs. As a result, non-Indians usually learn directly, or indirectly, not to be too inquisitive regarding the Pueblo religion, and in some cases, the culture—since it's difficult to separate the culture from religion.

Lee: Exactly. I'm not sure if we were ever given explicit instructions as to what was enough or too far. Religious stuff was always off limits. With some stories you just had to be cautious of how you approached the lessons. But if things were already written down or an elder guest spoke of certain things or told certain stories, then we were able to discuss it later on.

Jeanette: So, Gilbert and Lee, what I heard you say leads into what was in the course content. On talking about the tribal government, community development and the historical, that is what the young people need to know to be culturally literate Laguna members. But then when it enters into the religious realm, the traditional realm, then that is separated out into the family, or talked about with the approval of an elder. Essentially, there's a clear delineation between what would be introduced and discussed in the cultural class versus what is in the community as knowledge.

Gilbert: Right, right.

Teaching—Reaching Kids and Being Creative

Jeanette: I would like to move into the area of pedagogy. Lee, you've already mentioned that it is not just your typical written work, but it's also drawing or a creative sense of imagining the future. You spoke of watching for what the students reacted to and how you framed the involvement of the class. What were other ideas around pedagogy, or ways of teaching, including your philosophy and how this should be done?

Lee: I was such a novice when I began teaching the course. I had done writing workshops for high school and middle school students, so I had a sense of what they were interested in and how they would react to it. But coming into class, it was a lot of trial and error. It was trying to figure out how to reach kids on a daily basis, as teaching always is.

My philosophy was to get the kids to think and to be able to draw out their strengths and skills, while at the same time building upon the things that they needed, especially in writing. I told this to all the kids: "If I give you an assignment and you can come up with something better, and it's going to meet the qualifications, then you can do it. But you have to be able to explain to me why you want to do it." This approach was to build those critical thinking skills—those alternative and creative thinking skills. I had one student who was an excellent artist, so he gave me a separate assignment when we were studying the Pueblo Revolt. He said, "I want to draw a flag." And I said "So what about it?" The student answered, "Propaganda!" because the assignment was to write a speech as if you were Po'pay and you were trying to get people to join you in revolt. We went through various activities and most of the kids wrote and gave speeches. To the artistic student, I said, "Draw me a propaganda poster, as if you were doing that," and he did. He looked up *propaganda* and did research into World War I and World War II and the propaganda posters from that time. He drew me a *rally to our side* or *fight for us* sort of poster. He demonstrated his knowledge through a different form than the typical writing project.

Jeanette: That fits right in with CRT. Critical race theorists, such as Solórzano and Yosso (2001), speak to the importance of fighting off the cultural deficit theory placed on Students of Color; that is, deficit by looking at their background and suggesting what they don't have as compared to the dominating society. However, you are identifying what they are good at as a way for them to *read the world*. In your pedagogy you "recreate, and recover knowledge and art in communities of color" (Solórzano & Yosso, 2001, p. 36).

Lee: What I wanted to do was figure out more ways to draw them out, but it really was something they were engaged in. The philosophy behind it was to work with each one of the students because not everybody is going to be the same. They are not going to work at the same pace. If you want to be an artist, I'm going to focus on letting you be an artist. You're going to have to learn how to write, but I'm going to let you do more on the artistic side.

For me, in terms of the pedagogy, it's that cutting edge stuff that everybody is realizing now, that we're using the various aspects that the students all have: the tactile, the kinesthetic, the visual, the auditory, and so on. I very much found in my classes that the visual was very, very important. I have distinct memories of when I had four or five power point presentations over the course of the year covering some major issues or was showing them photographs. Nobody was talking; they were engaged and they were taking notes.

My work is student-focused. I really tried to give every kid that opportunity, plus a lot of fun and games, a lot of experiential learning. While we were studying education I had them make a board game called *Escape from Boarding School*, so they all made little board games how they would escape from the boarding school. We started at Carlisle[12] [Pennsylvania], and home was Laguna or Paguate, or wherever it was. They had to make their own die or they spun a wheel; it was great, they all loved it. That was one of the assignments that I designed that I knew I would use again. The experiential, the immediacy of the assignment: they could see that it matched up with something. So it was not writing for writing's sake, or drawing for drawing's sake, although we did match it with that. Those were the most successful assignments.

The course was also very organic and very flexible. I mean, there were times when I had my curriculum, my lesson plan for the day, and I would look at it and go, "You know what, just given our conversation from the day before, I want to throw this in here." Or, I would read something I would find particularly interesting and integrate it into our lesson.

Importance of the Laguna Culture and History Course to the Community

Jeanette: Gilbert, as the former Superintendent of the Pueblo of Laguna Department of Education, what was the importance of this class or such a class?

Gilbert: On a scale of 1-10 with 10 being the highest, I would put it right there at 9 or 10 because it was very important. It gives the students the orientation to know who they are, where they come from. It connects the stories they hear from their family members. The Pueblo is in the midst of a whole economic development trend. What road do we want to go down? Is it always going to just be casino gaming? Are there other things you can do? That is something that is their future; so I think the course helps with that as well. They're going to hear about issues of mineral deposits with the Jackpile Mine. Now we've got the water situation because of it—some of it is contaminated, you know. What about even the air space that we have over head? All of those things are coming up. So I think if they have the orientation to the basics, it just helps them so much more in the process of how they look at things. We shared with them the history *textbook*, so to speak, of what we know of our community, economic development, and tribal government. All of that is rich and is knowledge that we should all be sharing because it gives us a better understanding of development, where we've been, and what we've learned.

Jeanette: Lee, you were talking about how you framed self-determination and sovereignty, about destiny and people deciding for the community. Would you say the Laguna History and Culture class in itself was an act of self-determination?

Lee: Yes, and I hope that it continues. I think it is an act of self-determination much in the same way the middle school got started, and the control of the elementary school was taken by the [Laguna] Department of Education. And I think that that class is one of those ways of saying, "This is important and it's important to know your history," as much as it is important to learn American history. In teaching our history the students learn the intricacies that I think are important. Others might try to cover it in a New Mexico history class but they never do it comprehensively or from our perspective. But I don't even know we can ever do Laguna history justice like that either, because you only have nine months to learn it. But I do think it is that step towards determining what we want to learn and what's important to our continued survival.

Contextual Challenges and the Laguna History and Culture Class

Jeanette: Was the course designed for all the high school students, or for those at the junior level or the senior level? Who got to take the course?

Gilbert: When we started this idea, it was focused at the high school level. I think the content would basically address any group, but that's who it was focused on.

Jeanette: Is there someone teaching it now?

Gilbert: No, it was pulled back from the offerings at the end of 2004-2005 because, from what I could see, it was real shaky at that point. The schools were focused on NCLB and all of that—it wasn't necessarily lining up with their NCLB focus and goals. Also, we didn't really have a person to work on developing the course.

Another issue is that it looked like the school used it as another way to put just any students into it. We had non-Indian students that the school was asking to have placed in there. You always have that option because it's a public school, but I don't know if it was as much for the students wanting to learn as it was a place for putting students that the school had no other place for.

We ended up going down to the middle school level with the course as well. However, I felt like I didn't want to go down that road if we didn't have the support of the staff and the financial support to really develop a quality curriculum. I didn't want it to be a dumping ground such as to the effect of "You have this class, we're helping you out, so take these students." The whole thing had been falling apart so I felt that we should pull it back and do some work on it first and then go back to it at some point.

Lee: Yes, that was sometimes a point of frustration for me because a lot of times kids that didn't necessarily want to take the class were thrown into the class, but we still tried to accommodate them by teaching them the history. But then again, some of them really wanted to take it. I had some kids that were really interested in it and we tried to make it fun and exciting for them. But, right, it was an elective. We were really working on trying to get it as a history credit.

Jeanette: Okay, I'm hearing you say the course didn't have a high status within the school or the district, as compared to being a course such as a calculus class. It was only an elective for students who had room for electives, it wasn't a required history course.

Gilbert: No, it was not required at the time. In time that would be the idea, that it would become a credit for a history or culture requirement or something like that.

Jeanette: Why do you think it was not a history credit class? What would the context for that be?

Lee: There was a lot of support, and at the same time there was not a lot of support. Sometimes it just falls into where they'll [the district officials] say "That's a great idea," but then it never gets implemented. So not getting into it too deep, I don't think there was a hesitation, I think there was a sense that they have the Acoma language class in there and there was a big push for that, and I think that if we had made a major push for the history class it would probably have been accepted. While the class was going, I don't know if Laguna-Acoma was ready to put something like that into place due to the flux in the administration, at that time there were four principals in four years, and the school was on probation for not meeting AYP. The school had to have this class specifically for the middle school; it was part of being on probation. I came here to teach first at the middle school, and then the course was moved to the high school. I don't know if the school officials made an actual decision, I think they just included the class for high school students to add another elective and to appease community members who were frustrated that Acoma had a language and culture class for high school students and so should Laguna. I didn't have much insight into the behind the scenes decisions.

Gilbert: There are approximately four levels for schools not meeting AYP, so schools are notified and expected to show improvement over a number of years. The term *probation* is used to refer to schools in this situation. I believe at the time, one of requirements for middle schools was a unit in Southwest history, which usually consisted of standard information straight out of textbooks. The course taught by Lee was of interest to students because it was about their people, community, land, and history so it more than fulfilled the unit in Southwest history. I think the school administration saw this as an opportunity for creating another elective for students as the school struggled for balance in their course offerings.

Continuing the Work

Gilbert: We said we would develop our content as we went along. I think we did that; but again, we really didn't have someone with the background or training to develop the course. So, I think Lee did an outstanding job. Now we have a lot of material, but we did not have the framework to specifically identify the objectives to line the course up to meet the state benchmarks. But, that could be done now. I think the fact that we taught the course two-and-a-half academic years shows that we have a lot of information to share. We have not been able to get back to it, to really work on the curriculum piece; that is the next step we have to do.

In terms of sovereignty, I'm not sure how much we did specifically with the sovereignty piece. That is so important. I think that is one of the areas that we need a real emphasis on.

Lee: The course is still in flux. We still want to work on it and get it even more solid, get it to becoming, almost, an independent [class] so that we can take the curriculum and pull out the lesson plans, and use them in the classes that they are teaching.

Another direction is the language; the kids wanted to learn the Laguna language. If I had known the language we would have taught it. When I had guest speakers come in, they would teach some of it to the kids and the kids would pick up words here and there. People here at the Pueblo have been working with the New Mexico Public Education Department so we will be able to certify our *own* to teach the language class at the high school. With that, we may be able to get a language class or we may be able to blend the two, in terms of the history and culture with the language piece. The kids wanted the language; they kept calling it "the language and culture class," and I was like, "No, it is a history and culture class." But we could not support the language piece in the class. We'll see what happens with that.

Vested in the Force of Our Own People

Jeanette: Within academic circles, and within the writings of Indigenous scholars, such as those in the *For Indigenous Eyes Only* text (Wilson & Yellow Bird, 2005), issues of colonization and decolonization have been continuously discussed. Have those terms or concepts entered into discussions here in the community?

Gilbert: In my work in the community and with the staff and educators, we don't talk about *colonization* per say. It might be talked about in terms of oppression, but not colonization.

Lee: In the general sense it is there, but we don't use the term, *colonization*. It has been more, "We need to teach our own history; they're not getting their history, and they're not going to get this history." Prior to the years that we had the course, people did not get that detailed history. They might know that the mine was open and that the railroad came through, but they didn't know the origins of those things. That is what gets devalued, that intelligence. It hasn't been discussed in terms of colonization and decolonization; it has been more within the discourse of what *we* want to teach our people and our kids. The issue is: How do they incorporate that into the curriculum within the school so that the students have that knowledge? It is critical. The terms haven't been used but the issues around our history in the curriculum, identity and representation have been addressed.

Jeanette: When looking at issues around, specifically, the language, self-determination, sovereignty, colonization, was any of that in the course?

Gilbert: I talked with Lee about it and I think he hit some of those areas, particularly around the tribal governance piece and the community piece.

Jeanette: Talking about the periods of colonization and entering into using the word *colonization* is controversial for a lot of people. Was there anything that was off limits? Being that the Spanish Land Grant is right here, and you have the Anglo community, and looking at all the history that was, in many ways, very ugly, were there things that you had to tiptoe around? Or, did you just go ahead and enter into discussions?

Lee: In terms of the history, it was entering into discussions. I don't think I ever tiptoed around anything. I laid out the facts. I had Land Grant kids; I had Hispanics in the class; it wasn't an exclusionary class. I taught that this was the way it was, and you have to understand that this was the mindset at the time. If someone was to take some of those actions now, we would say, "This is awful; don't do that," and try to stop them. But looking at it in the past we still want to say the same thing. But, it is done. We can tiptoe around it or we can say, "This is what happened. It may have been your grandparents, but it's not you." You can't avoid it; I mean, what do you say, "Shhh, not here" and ignore it?

Jeanette: In terms of the content you talked about colonization, did you come into the areas of sovereignty and self-determination?

Lee: We got into it especially with the government; that was really something that we stressed. Sovereignty was a very difficult concept for the kids to understand. What does sovereignty mean? What does self-determination mean? How far does it go? I stressed to the kids that as Indian people they are independent, that they're able to make decisions, and that they need to help their community so it becomes successful and self-sustaining. That's what I tried to boil it down to.

When I think of sovereignty and self-determination it's the fact that we don't have to take handouts from the government. That we get to choose what we do with our schools, that we've set the standards, and that we've decided what we want to see our students accomplish. It's also that we don't have someone regulating what we're able to build and what we're not able to build, where we're able to do gaming compacts, and all these various things. It's truly self-determination and it's truly sovereignty only if it's desired by *our own* people, vested in the force of our own people.

References

Cheromiah, N. (2004). *Laguna History: First edition*. Laguna, NM: private printing.

Fixico, D. L. (2003). *An American Indian mind in a linear world: American Indian studies and traditional knowledge*. New York: Routledge.

Meyer, M. A. (2002, November). Keynote Address presented at the 33rd annual National

Indian Education Association Convention, Albuquerque, NM.

Solórzano, D. G., & Yosso, T. J. (2001). From racial stereotyping and deficit discourse toward a critical race theory in teacher education. *Multicultural Education, 9*(1), 2-8.

Wilson, A. W., & Yellow Bird, M. (Eds.). (2005). *For Indigenous eyes only: A decolonization handbook.* Santa Fe, NM: School of America Research Press.

Notes

[1] Uranium was discovered on Laguna lands in the 1950s prompting the Pueblo to lease its lands for mining to take advantage of mining royalties and new revenue opportunities. The Jackpile Uranium Mine was the largest open-pit mine in the world and operated from 1953-1982, employing approximately 500 tribal members. At first the uranium industry brought employment and economic prosperity to community members, however, after the closing of the mines in 1982, the lasting legacy of the enterprise is the devastating health issues and contamination of the People's land and water sources. See Eichstaedt (1994), *If You Poison Us: Uranium and Native Americans*, mention is made of the Jackpile Mine reclamation efforts, pp. 147-149.

[2] After years of enduring the Spanish colonizers taking over Pueblo lands and exploiting and killing the Pueblo Peoples, a resistance movement was waged to drive out the Spanish in 1680. Po'pay, from Ohkay Owingeh Pueblo (formerly known as San Juan Pueblo), is credited as being a central organizer of the resistance. See Sando & Agoyo (2005).

[3] The Long Walk was the forced relocation of the Navajo from their homelands to Bosque Redondo in 1864. The removal of the Diné People was conducted by the U.S. military and hundreds died as a result of the forced migration and poor conditions where they were held prisoner. See Denetdale & Rosier (2007).

[4] Delpit (1993) discusses the importance of acknowledging students' home or community knowledge and ways of being while adding new forms of knowledge and skills from the larger society so students have access to the "culture of power" (p. 24).

[5] Within the NCLB Act *migrant, Indian, economically disadvantaged, disabled, and limited English proficient* students are specifically identified (NCLB, 2001).

[6] both Nieto (2004) and Valencia (1997) discuss the deficit model which serves to blame particular students and families for educational failure or non-success.

[7] Adams (1995) and Szasz (1999) provide an in-depth discussion on the historical impact of Westernized schooling on Native Peoples and illuminate assimilationist ideologies, practices, policies and law.

[8] A number of authors address this issue; see Garcia (2008), Lomawaima & McCarty (2006), McCarty (2009), National Indian Education Association (2010), Patrick (2008), and Tippeconnic (2003).

[9] Cochiti Pueblo scholar, Joseph Suina (1992), in his article "Pueblo Secrecy Result of Intrusions," explains the secrecy surrounding Pueblo religion and the historical conditions that made secrecy necessary.

[10] See Smith (1999) for a discussion on the exploitation of Westernized research methodologies on Indigenous Peoples.

[11] See Carpenter, Katyal and Riley (2009) for a legal discussion of intangible Indigenous cultural property rights which pushes back on the European heritage of "ownership" and "title" in property law.

[12] The first boarding school for American Indian children was established in Carlisle, Pennsylvania, in 1879. The school was part of the United States federal government policy of assimilating Indigenous Peoples into the dominating society. Native children between the

ages of 8 and 25 were taken hundreds and even thousands of miles from their tribal nations and communities, usually through methods of coercion, and stripped of their cultures in an attempt to blot out any remnants of tribal identity. Christianity was used as a primary tool in this cultural genocide through a curriculum that emphasized all that was deemed "good" in White society. Native knowledges and languages were degraded, silenced, forgotten, replaced with what was valued and privileged in the dominating White society. The children, like their curriculum, were standardized. Psychological conditioning occurred at the boarding schools, conditioning to make the children want to forget who they were and where they came from. See Adams (1995), *Education for Extinction: American Indians and the boarding school experience, 1875-1928* for a comprehensive examination of Carlisle and other Indian boarding schools.

CHAPTER TEN
RECLAIMING THE LAGUNA WORLDVIEW

Jeanette Haynes Writer
Lee Francis, IV
Gilbert Sanchez

A course involving Laguna history and culture is important for the Pueblo of Laguna on a number of levels: 1) it validates the role of the Pueblo and its people in New Mexico history and in contemporary times; 2) it provides context for discussion on various issues of importance to the community, for example, language change, social justice, economic development and governance; 3) it helps counter assaults on the culture and language of the community, ensuring cultural continuance; and 4) it engenders pride in youth of being Laguna and of being Native American and, therefore, facilitates their development as culturally literate Laguna members and leaders which supports the on-going well-being of their community.

Consider the following case in point: the 2006 Florida Education Omnibus Act/bill signed by Governor Jeb Bush proclaimed history texts as objective documents containing historical facts, regardless of the historical and contemporary biases existing in these or school textbooks based on these (State of Florida, 2010). Challenges to, or negotiations of, the socially constructed perspectives in the textbooks are not an option. All in all, we maintain that courses that center tribal histories from the Native frame of reference are necessary for cultural continuance and are especially important in light of the denial of American Indian genocide, the continued suppression of Native Peoples' history in both public and education discourse, and legislative attacks on Indigenous Peoples' truth telling in educational contexts.

Another alarming example of such silencing and continued colonization is the 2008 Arizona Senate Bill 1108, which was eventually revised as House Bill 2281 and signed in to law by Governor Jan Brewer in May 2010. Developed and proposed by Republican Representative Russell Pearce, in the Arizona House of Representatives, April 2008, Senate Bill 1108 aimed to abolish the Movimiento Estudiantil Chicano de Aztlan (MEChA) and Mexican-American study programs, with Indigenous students, teachers and faculty becoming a target as well. Moreover, Pearce's[1] proposed legislation demanded that,

> A public school in this state shall not include within the program of instruction any courses, classes or school sponsored activities that promote, assert as truth or feature as an exclusive focus any political, religious, ideological or cultural beliefs or values that denigrate, disparage or overtly encourage dissent from the values of American democracy and western civilization, including democracy, capitalism, pluralism and religious toleration. (Arizona State Legislature, 2008).

This bill stipulated that tax payer dollars could not be utilized in the *denigration* of American values or Western civilization. Should textbooks and/or other teaching materials be found (i.e., *interpreted*) to be anti-American, the State Superintendent of Public Instruction would have authority to confiscate such materials. Furthermore, the bill prohibited public schools, community colleges, and universities from sponsoring or granting official status to campus organizations "based in whole or in part on race-based criteria" (Arizona State Legislature, 2008), such as an American Indian Student Association. Yet organizations based on political affiliation, such as the Young Democrats or College Republicans, as well as those based on religious or gender affiliation (e.g., Campus crusade for Christ), would be permitted and privileged under the proposed bill. The proposed bill was passed by the State House Appropriations Committee in April 2008 and advanced to the full House and Senate for a vote. It did not, however, proceed to the 2008 legislative year. Nonetheless, ideologically similar legislation was re-introduced and eventually signed into law in 2010 with House Bill 2281. In Section 15-112, subsection A, this law prohibited courses that (1) promote the overthrow of the United States government; (2) promote resentment toward a race or class of people; (3) are designated primarily for pupils of a particular ethnic group; (4) and advocate ethnic solidarity instead of treatment of pupils as individuals[2] (Arizona State Legislature, 2010, p. 1). Should a violation be identified by the Arizona State Board of Education, or the Superintendent of Public Instruction, the Department of Education may withhold up to 10% of the monthly state aid after notifying the school district or charter school and after noncompliance of 60 days.

This law is a particularly important example of contradiction and oppression. It clearly reflects oppression because its enforcement is driven by punitive compliance, based on the privileged perceptions of those in power. In terms of contradiction, the law exempts courses for Native American students, a particular ethnic group that is protected by federal law, as well as discussions regarding the Jewish Holocaust. In particular, these exemptions create a contradiction in terms of the wording of the law, which prohibits "resentment toward a race or class of people" (Arizona State Legislature, 2010, p. 1). Discussing the genocide of Native people by whites, or the genocide of Jewish people by Germans, could potentially cause resentment and qualify as *threatening content*. Even so, the law itself is a threat to those who practice historical literacy by composing counterstories that challenge the typical master narrative privileged within the standardized curriculum. It is clear that the introduction of the 2008 bill and the current law serve as evidence, enactment, and protection of white privilege—where whiteness and its encompassing history are normalized, and in terms of academic literacy, are standardized. Such legal action serves to promote and function as a guard for an *official* history or curriculum. In the process, colonization is sponsored, advanced and legislated. Native People's truth-telling of their histories and experiences are silenced and essentially outlawed through legislated educational censorship. Divergent voices are positioned as anti-American; thus these are simply assumed to be a threat. The master narrative of Manifest Destiny is so ingrained within the mainstream American consciousness that any challenge to it or any counterstory presented along with it may be interpreted as an attempt to overthrow the U.S. government or translated into a resentment of Europeans or their white American descendants (i.e., white guilt), thus construed as the law's "resentment toward a race or class of people" (Arizona State Legislature, 2010, p. 1).

In reality, the *Indian Wars* did not end in the late 1800s: these continue in terms of the wars that are waged over educational curriculum, ideologies, laws, and policies. In the era of the *reading wars* and the NCLB Act, literacy has been conceptualized as the domain of the written word. Oral traditions and reading the world (Freire & Macedo, 1987) are not worth mentioning in the text of the Act or the spirit of the law. The focus on *intervention* and *improvement* is positioned in situating the Other as having inherent deficits and being in need of assistance. Literacy is contextualized in the Westernized production of education within the paradigm of *whiteness*. *Whiteness* and its associated values are privileged and not examined within NCLB; rather, it is *naturalized* in the process of the Act and its directives.

Being forced to utilize the written words of others as the only acceptable form of literacy serves to silence Indigenous histories, our counterstories, and operates to establish and maintain the existence and privilege of the master narrative. This, then, institutes what Jeanette has termed the *privilege of non-knowledge*" that is, "the belief that no other story or history—*or ways of teaching and learning*—exists than what is written or documented on the printed page" (Haynes Writer, 2012, p. 63).[3] Employing the mantra of *scientifically-based research*, the privilege of non-knowledge is the very foundation of NCLB's conceptualization of literacy, curriculum, pedagogy, and standardized tests, not just for Native Peoples but for a multitude of diverse communities.

With this said, we identify here another level of importance of Native-centered courses such as the Laguna History and Culture class. The creation of such courses operates as a way of speaking back to the privilege of non-knowledge. Euro-centric histories situated within a Westernized education system has legislated and manifested white privilege, effectively imposing white privilege on children and youth all across the country because they often do not have access—are not permitted access—to more accurate, pluralistic narratives of history of all United States citizens. The result has been, specifically for Native Peoples and communities, the silencing of Indigenous histories while systematically manufacturing invisibility on the one hand and, on the other, continuing to stereotype Native people. It is up to Native communities to push back against the NCLB-situated master narrative to develop culturally literate and historically literate community members.

Further, Native-centered courses offered within Westernized schools advance what Yosso (2005) names as *community cultural wealth*. Within the CRT framework, community cultural wealth resists the assumption that Students of Color come to school with only deficits that need to be filled or corrected with the dominating societal academic knowledge, skills and ways of being. Students instead come to school with community cultural wealth which is "an array of knowledge, skills, abilities and contacts possessed and utilized by Communities of Color to survive and resist macro and micro-forms of oppression" (Yosso, 2005, p. 77). Native-centered courses, such as the Laguna History and Culture class taught by Laguna members, highlight the existence of the community cultural wealth and create space for it in the school setting.

The course may serve as a model for other tribal communities in their endeavors to provide culturally relevant and tribally-centered education for their students[4] by helping them to understand their successes and counteracting the opposition to offering a course similar to this. The focus of the Laguna History and Culture course was middle and high school-aged students. Although such a course is focused in the context of a school-based course, it could also be enacted in teaching and learning outside of school (i.e. after school programs or summer learning opportunities). Questions that tribal officials, educators, and community members might ask to determine if a course is warranted in their community are:

1. What is being taught about a tribal community's history, specifically, or Native history, in general, and who is doing the teaching?
2. What kinds of partnerships exist between the local schools serving the tribal community and the various community/tribal programs?
3. What kinds of youth programs exist within the community and schools to provide an enriched cultural curriculum and youth leadership development?
4. What is the fluency rate of Native speakers in their tribal heritage language and are the youth learning the language and culture in ways and to levels that ensure cultural continuance?

In sum, the crucial point of such a course is that the perspective privileged in framing the curriculum is that of the tribal community, which occurs by community members taking part in the development and teaching of the course.

The teaching of the Laguna History and Culture class was ended due to the various challenges discussed earlier by Gilbert and Lee. The challenges or issues faced in offering the course included not having a project director to support Lee's work—one person could not do it all. Because of this, ongoing curriculum and material development was lacking and a thorough evaluation process was not created even though it was discussed. Working within a public school was extremely difficult considering district administrative and localized or federal education policy issues; school administration and staff issues; logistics and time needed for lesson planning; and space issues. A primary obstacle was that additional resources were not available to fully support the course's creation nor were resources made available to sustain the project.

Personally speaking, the development of the Laguna History and Culture class was important for both Lee and Gilbert. Lee asserts that the process of creating the class was necessary and helpful in defining his career path. He discussed how the creation of the class assisted in his understanding that culture is not simply language and religion, but that it is all the things that Laguna people are and were. Lee found it imperative to have support from the school system when trying to create something like the Laguna History and Culture course, instead he found that actual participation and reflection with the administration was something that was lacking during his time teaching the class.

Gilbert also found that creating the class was a great learning experience for him. He acknowledges the gracious support from Lee's father, a professor, with the planning and process for starting the course; the collaboration and Dr. Francis' educational credentials brought credibility to the project. Although he had little tangible support, Gilbert did not allow the lack of resources to halt the process of creating the course. He also approached the project from an assets perspective by capitalizing on Laguna community cultural wealth. The people of the community presented the background to the course's curricular topics situated within the Laguna culture, history, language and people—community members were invested in the course along with Gilbert and Lee.

Even though the course is no longer taught, our work together on the chapter was the result of its continued reverberations. As Gilbert, Lee and Jeanette continue decolonization work within themselves and in their work with Native communities, the course serves as an example of what is possible when Indigenous people create spaces for Native perspectives in the context of schooling and work together in collaboration to ensure cultural continuance. Transforming oppressive structures and re-writing/righting history is an achievable and necessary action. We see this in how Gilbert envisioned the Laguna History and Culture class through a lens of sovereignty and self-determination. We see this in how Lee dismissed deficit perspectives of the students' abilities as he conceptualized the curriculum and while he situated himself in a strengths-based pedagogy. And on another front, in her work with pre-service and in-service teachers within the teacher education program at her university, Jeanette utilizes Critical Race Theory and TribalCrit to help the teachers understand how educational theory and practice are used to subordinate Indigenous Peoples and how accessing divergent stories opens possibilities within the educational arena.

References

Arizona State Legislature (2008). Proposed House of Representatives amendments to S.B. 1108.
http://www.azleg.gov/FormatDocument.asp?inDoc=/legtext/48leg/2R/proposed/H.1108_RP2.DOC.htm (retrieved August 8, 2013)

Arizona State Legislature (2010). House Bill 2281. Retrieved from
http://www.azleg.gov/legtext/49leg/2r/bills/hb2281s.pdf

Freire, P., & Macedo, D. (1987). *Literacy: Reading the word and the world.* New York: Bergin & Garvey.

Haynes Writer, J. (2012). The savage within: No child left behind—again, and again, and again. In B. J. Klug (Ed.), *Standing together: American Indian education as culturally responsive pedagogy* (pp. 55-70). Lanham, MD: R&L Education.

State of Florida, Department of State. (2010). Chapter 2006-74, House Bill No. 7087. http://laws.flrules.org/2006/74. (retrieved August 8, 2013)

Yosso, T. J. (2005). Whose culture has capital? A critical race theory discussion of community cultural wealth. *Race and Ethnicity in Education, 8*(1), 69-91.

Notes

[1] In 2006, Pearce was confronted with circulating an article to supporters through e-mail from National Alliance, a white separatist group ("Arizona lawmaker circulated," 2006).

[2] Many Native people give great emphasis on their membership within their tribe(s), tribal community or family. As such, the legislative act of enforcing individual identity is a form of whitestreaming (Denis, 1997) and assimilation.

[3] Jeanette introduced the term "privilege of non-knowledge" in her (2012) chapter, "The Savage Within: No Child Left Behind—Again, and Again, and Again," to describe her experience in school with teachers who denied her knowledge of tribal or Native history. Due to their lack of knowledge and their power over her or other students, these teachers possessed a privilege to deny or ignore the shared information or knowledge as valuable or even valid. These teachers, through their non-knowledge, had power and privilege to disadvantage or withhold opportunity from Jeanette or other students like her, or altogether silence students in their challenge of the master narrative or presentation of counterstories.

[4] It is important to note two examples of Native history being formally taught. The first is the Montana Indian Education for All Act, which is a state education law developed out of collaboration between Montana's tribal communities and the Montana Department of Education to ensure that Montana Native history is taught and taught accurately to all of Montana's public school students (see Carjuzaa, Jetty, Munson & Veltkamp, 2010). The second example is the tribal history course taught through the Cherokee Nation. This course was developed to ensure that Cherokee Nation tribal employees and tribal members have a complete and accurate knowledge base. This course was offered throughout the Cherokee Nation tribal jurisdictional area and across the United States, due to the diaspora of the Cherokee People, in areas where Cherokee Nation citizens reside.

CHAPTER ELEVEN
LAGUNA CULTURAL LITERACY

Jeanette Haynes Writer
Lee Francis, IV
Gilbert Sanchez

Drawing from the theoretical framework of TribalCrit, one speaks to and through the historical condition of colonization when speaking of and about Indigenous experiences. As a tenet of TribalCrit, we understand that colonization as well as the resistance waged against colonization are salient threads woven within the stories that Indigenous Peoples tell (Brayboy, 2005). To "recognize the direct link between what goes on in schools and the politics of Indian-white relations" (Marker, 1997, p. 18), we specifically identify and discuss the link between the historical turbulence among the Native and Anglo (and Hispanic) communities, nationally and locally, and the contested territories within the schools Laguna students attend. As told through our story, colonization, in both historical and present form, was named, confronted and challenged through the development and teaching of the Laguna History and Culture class.

Our chapter provides other Native communities and educators a model of *possibility* and a sharing of *lessons learned* which fulfills the activist dimension of CRT and TribalCrit. The vision for, creation and instruction of, and results from the course are not put aside as memory of a few; these are carried through this story into public academic discourse so others may share in the broadening of the view of literacy. Through our work together on this essay, we maintain that literacy encompasses multiple forms; it is not limited to NCLB's version of *literacy equals the printed word*. Literacy is enacted in communities through the stories told by elders and adults to the young people; it is reading the world in ways where oppressions are questioned and challenged; it is alive in the engagement of young people exerting their voices and taking action as tribal members; and, it is enacted in community with each other.

To remedy the discounting of Indigenous knowledge and history, or in this case, specifically Laguna knowledge and history within the public school setting, the workings of colonization are understood and named, facilitating change so sovereignty and self-determination will be upheld in full effect. By telling the story of the historical oppression of Indigenous Peoples, and the experience of Laguna educators in developing a class to educate the Pueblo's young people to what is important to the community, we become literate in reference to colonization and decolonization. Our work together, through our storytelling, assisted in the development of a lens to recognize and to name colonization in a critical manner. Drawing upon the framework and words of Solórzano and Yosso (2001), we look at our work here, together, as "a social justice project that attempts to link theory with practice, scholarship with teaching, and the academy with the *community*" [emphasis ours] (p. 31).

In close, we challenge the concept of literacy as put forth by the NCLB Act that literacy only occurs by means of the written word. We take back from E. D. Hirsch, Jr. (1988) the concept of cultural literacy to re-appropriate and recast it here: a person who knows her or his Laguna history and culture is one who is culturally literate. Colonization of Native Peoples continues by valuing only and forcing us to use only the written word—the written words of non-Native others—thereby extinguishing our critical thinking and tribal histories and knowledge foundations. We maintain that the oral tradition is a valid way of *reading the world* (Macedo & Freire, 1987). It serves as the basis for the exercise of sovereignty and self-determination by Native Nations, as evidenced through the development and teaching of the Laguna History and Culture class, to facilitate and support Indigenous youth in developing into culturally literate tribal members. It is only through this type of literacy development in our young people that our Native Nations will continue to exist and thrive.

References

Brayboy, B. M. J. (2005, December).Toward a tribal critical race theory in education. *The Urban Review, 37*(5), 425-446.

Freire, P., & Macedo, D. (1987). *Literacy: Reading the word and the world.* New York: Bergin & Garvey.

Hirsch, E. D., Jr. (1988). *Cultural literacy: What every American needs to know.* New York: Vintage Books.

Marker, M. (1997, Spring). Indian education in the Pacific Northwest: The missing research. *Tribal College Journal, 9*(4), 16-21.

Solórzano, D. G., & Yosso, T. J. (2001). From racial stereotyping and deficit discourse toward a critical race theory in teacher education. *Multicultural Education, 9*(1), 2-8.

CONCLUSION

CHAPTER TWELVE
A GIFT AT A MOST OPPORTUNE TIME

Donna E. Muncey, Los Angeles Unified School District

Being asked to read these three extraordinary studies was a gift given to me at a most opportune time.

The opportune time

As the 2013-2014 school year drew to a close, there were no signs that as a country we were anywhere near the central promise of No Child Left Behind (NCLB; 2001). That promise, you will recall, was that by the end of this past year, and after enacting scores of regulatory changes linked to the NCLB version of the Elementary and Secondary Education Act (ESEA), 100 percent of the nation's students would be proficient or better on federally-mandated, state-developed English Language Arts, mathematics and science tests. In fact, far from administering this final round of testing, and taking stock of our cumulative progress towards the 100 percent mark, some states, including California—the state where I currently live and work—spent the recently completed spring testing season piloting a whole new testing regime (i.e., on-line, soon-to-be computer-adapted, Common Core State Standards assessments). In effect, the state decided—with federal approval, of course—to pass on administering that final assessment of their more than a decade-long calendar of planned increments in testing success that was to herald the arrival of universal proficiency.

On the one hand, there was no need to administer that final test to conclude that we as a state, but more importantly the nation as a whole, are nowhere near the goal of universal proficiency, no matter what standard of proficiency had been articulated in each state. There do appear to be glimmers of understanding that without a common definition of *universal proficiency* this charge has been something of a chimera[1] from the get-go.

At the same time and after apparent widespread agreement with the next new approach to creating a national set of standards (the Common Core) and assessments, as states began inching toward implementing these new standards and assessing students against aligned tests, discord about the need for, content of, and appropriateness of those proposed common standards has intensified nationally. Occurring as it is during a very highly politicized and polarized period in our recent history, the escalating rhetoric about what all students should know and be able to do—at least as instantiated in national, state and/or local standards—is not exactly generating a productive conversation about this most important topic.

Which takes me to the unexpected gift of having the opportunity to read the three studies featured in this book.

The gift

It is an incredible gift to present such rich and thought-provoking studies about critical literacy to us at this moment in time. Each study offers an opportunity to learn from a central and critical educative topic: family child care and the education of family child care providers, Pueblo of Laguna's history, local conceptions of cultural literacy and their *place* in the education of the Pueblo's students, and the learning and sense-making an educational community can do through creating poetry, or other literary forms, and listening to, then interrogating, each other's creative writings.

The studies in this book remind us powerfully that there are multiple ways that all of us—children, parents, teachers, program administrators and other educational decision makers—learn or choose not to learn. The authors record efforts to present critical information and/or build comprehensive understanding that may well, but not always, lead to changes in behavior or willingness to accept or question current or past practice. These studies remind us that pre-packaged curriculum may get us part way to deeper learning and/or understanding, but that the kind of creation seen in the works of the students in Series Two, *Literacy Demands on New Mexico Teachers and Students*, are far more likely to emerge through the long, labor-intensive process described in the study than they are through programmed curriculum that rarely rises above the demand for recall in the responses to the questions it preposes for teachers to use in structured, whole-group or remedial sub-group, instruction.

The study *A Critical Literacy of Family Child Care: Policy, Practice and Self-Determination*, Series One, in particular, educated me about the challenge of addressing the issue itself through the careful description within the case, first, of who provides most of the child-care in the country and why. Then, the extremely thoughtful, iterative approach taken by the planners, coupled with the careful analysis of the feedback, both reflected the learner-centered approach to the work and revealed the increasing sense of the magnitude of the task being undertaken and the need to expand the planning to address the ever-broadening dimensions of the task. At each stage of the development, implementation, reflection, and revision—and counter to much of the literature about *helping* people learn to do something a state entity and/or funder wants done—the emphasis on listening to learn from and about what was or was not being taught and learned was highly welcomed by participants, also led to deeper understanding and provoked change to the plans that was perceived as both responsive and necessary. The authors wrote:

> With only a single story about family child care, there would not have been extensive discussion and reflection on the challenge of communicating explicitly with family members about fair business practice and its implications for ultimately meeting children's needs and providing ongoing child care; there would not have been sensitive and sophisticated dialogue about various issues of child abuse and neglect in terms of how to notice these as well as communicate accordingly; there would not have been clear and varied illustrations of acknowledging and responding accurately and directly to children's language and literacy. Listening to many stories made this possible. (p. 48).

In other words, as a result of listening to how participants were responding to the original instructional modules and to what they were saying was needed or were implying was missing through their questions and concerns, the next iteration of the training was stronger, richer, and more responsive to the needs and concerns expressed by the child care providers and reflective of the power of learning in community.

A similar outcome was evident through the use of poetry reading and writing in Series Two, *Literacy Demands on New Mexico Teachers and Students*. The engagement of the students—in two classes at one New Mexico school labeled by the state as *failing*—in the literacy work of creating meaning through writing about self, family, struggle and circumstance was both a lovely description of the emergence of writers, more specifically poets, and something of a repudiation of the idea that the school where these two classes were taught is *failing to adequately educate* its students. Through a writing process of drafting, sharing and reflecting and re-writing rooted in open and repeated feedback, the students in these classrooms became communities of writers who wrote, listened, shared their experiences and deepened their understanding through their participation in both speaking and listening. Their willingness to expand their community to include future teachers from a near-by university and later their families and friends spoke volumes about the meaning their written work had for them and their desire to share that work in community settings beyond the classroom walls.

Series Three, *Reading the (De)Colonized World: Cultural Literacy for Pueblo of Laguna Students*, challenges the reader to rethink every aspect of the notion of *cultural literacy* asserting:

> ...we challenge the concept of literacy as put forth by the NCLB Act that literacy only occurs by means of the written word. We take back from E. D. Hirsch, Jr. (1988) the concept of cultural literacy to re-appropriate and recast if here: a person who knows her or his Laguna history and culture is one who is culturally literate. Colonization of Native peoples continues by valuing only and forcing us to

use only the written word—the written words of non-Native others – extinguishing our critical thinking and tribal histories and knowledge foundations. We maintain that the oral tradition is a valid way of "reading the world" (Macedo & Freire, 1987). It serves as the basis for the exercise of sovereignty and self-determination by Native Nations, as evidenced through the development and teaching of the Laguna History and Culture class, to facilitate and support Indigenous youth in developing into culturally literate tribal members. It is only through this type of literacy development in our young people that our Native Nations will continue to exist and thrive. (p. 113)

Through a complex, multi-leveled analysis of the creation of a Laguna History and Culture class and the group's ongoing struggle to insure the survival of core components of Laguna culture and history, this case, too, argues that the successful creation, cultivation and maintenance of community is deeply dependent upon the approaches to learning offered and valued in its community's educative processes and institutions. In their case, a strong commitment to maintain an oral tradition, in addition to a written one, preserves the core communicative functions of listening and speaking in the creation and maintenance of their Native identity and sovereignty.

Final Reflection

I currently live in Los Angeles and work for the Los Angeles Unified School District, the second largest school district in the United States. Each of these cases resonated with me, not simply because of the connection to community that I see across them—which in the past was a strong research interest of mine—but also because while reading each of these there were direct applications to our ongoing work: (1) to improve teaching and learning for all of our students, (2) to more authentically engage parents and members of the community in our ongoing work and our planning for future improvement and opportunities for our more than half a million students and their families, and (3) to more respectfully, and with greater cultural sensitivity, reach out to acknowledge, engage, and learn from the cultural diversity in the many, varied communities that exist within the vast territory that our more than 900 schools serve. I look forward to using these cases with my team, our community partners, and others across Los Angeles as we continue our improvement work and transition to the next national wave of school reform and improvement.

Notes

[1] You choose the most appropriate definition: an imaginary monster compounded of incongruous parts or an illusion or fabrication of the mind, especially: an unrealizable dream (both of these definitions are excerpted from 2014 on-line Merriam Webster dictionary).

www.ingramcontent.com/pod-product-compliance
Lightning Source LLC
Chambersburg PA
CBHW070942040526
R18240200001BA/R182402PG44116CBX00015BA/1